HARRIET BEECHER STOWE

HARRIET BEECHER STOWE

ROBERT E. JAKOUBEK

CHELSEA HOUSE PUBLISHERS

PHILADELPHIA

CHELSEA HOUSE PUBLISHERS
EDITOR-IN-CHIEF: Nancy Toff
EXECUTIVE EDITOR: Remmel T. Nunn
MANAGING EDITOR: Karyn Gullen Browne
COPY CHIEF: Juliann Barbato
PICTURE EDITOR: Adrian G. Allen
ART DIRECTOR: Maria Epes
MANUFACTURING MANAGER: Gerald Levine

American Women of Achievement
SENIOR EDITOR: Constance Jones

STAFF FOR HARRIET BEECHER STOWE
ASSOCIATE EDITOR: Maria Behan
COPY EDITOR: Nicole Bowen
DEPUTY COPY CHIEF: Ellen Scordato
EDITORIAL ASSISTANT: Heather Lewis
PICTURE RESEARCHER: Susan Biederman
ASSISTANT ART DIRECTOR: Laurie Jewell
DESIGN: Design Oasis
ASSISTANT DESIGNER: Donna Sinisgalli
PRODUCTION COORDINATOR: Joseph Romano
COVER ILLUSTRATOR: Carol Malcolm

9

Library of Congress Cataloging in Publication Data

Jakoubek, Robert E.
Harriet Beecher Stowe/Robert E. Jakoubek.
p.   cm.—(American women of achievement)
Bibliography: p.
Includes index.
Summary: A biography of the author famous for the antislavery
novel Uncle Tom's Cabin, but who wrote other works presenting a
clear picture of nineteenth-century New England.
ISBN 1-55546-680-X
        0-7910-0423-6 (pbk.)
1. Stowe, Harriet Beecher, 1811–1896—Biography—Juvenile literature. 2. Authors, American—19th century—Biography—Juvenile
literature. 3. Abolitionists—United States—Biography—Juvenile literature. [1. Stowe, Harriet Beecher, 1811–1896. 2. Authors, American.]
I. Title. II. Series.
PS2956.J35 1989
813'.3—dc19   88-22862
[B]   CIP
[92]   AC

CONTENTS

WOMEN of ACHIEVEMENT

Abigail Adams
WOMEN'S RIGHTS ADVOCATE

Jane Addams
SOCIAL WORKER

Madeleine Albright
STATESWOMAN

Louisa May Alcott
AUTHOR

Marian Anderson
SINGER

Susan B. Anthony
WOMAN SUFFRAGIST

Ethel Barrymore
ACTRESS

Clara Barton
AMERICAN RED CROSS FOUNDER

Elizabeth Blackwell
PHYSICIAN

Pearl Buck
AUTHOR

Margaret Bourke-White
PHOTOGRAPHER

Rachel Carson
BIOLOGIST AND AUTHOR

Mary Cassatt
ARTIST

Hillary Rodham Clinton
FIRST LADY/ATTORNEY

Diana, Princess of Wales
HUMANITARIAN

Emily Dickinson
POET

Isadora Duncan
DANCER

Amelia Earhart
AVIATOR

Betty Friedan
FEMINIST

Althea Gibson
TENNIS CHAMPION

Helen Hayes
ACTRESS

Katharine Hepburn
ACTRESS

Anne Hutchinson
RELIGIOUS LEADER

Mahalia Jackson
GOSPEL SINGER

Helen Keller
HUMANITARIAN

Jeane Kirkpatrick
DIPLOMAT

Barbara McClintock
BIOLOGIST

Margaret Mead
ANTHROPOLOGIST

Edna St. Vincent Millay
POET

Agnes de Mille
CHOREOGRAPHER

Julia Morgan
ARCHITECT

Grandma Moses
PAINTER

Georgia O'Keeffe
PAINTER

Sandra Day O'Connor
SUPREME COURT JUSTICE

Rosie O'Donnell
ENTERTAINER/COMEDIENNE

Eleanor Roosevelt
DIPLOMAT AND HUMANITARIAN

Wilma Rudolph
CHAMPION ATHLETE

Gloria Steinem
FEMINIST

Harriet Beecher Stowe
AUTHOR AND ABOLITIONIST

Elizabeth Taylor
ACTRESS/ACTIVIST

Barbara Walters
JOURNALIST

Edith Wharton
AUTHOR

Phyllis Wheatley
POET

Babe Didrikson Zaharias
CHAMPION ATHLETE

"Remember the Ladies"

MATINA S. HORNER

Remember the Ladies." That is what Abigail Adams wrote to her husband John, then a delegate to the Continental Congress, as the Founding Fathers met in Philadelphia to form a new nation in March of 1776. "Be more generous and favorable to them than your ancestors. Do not put such unlimited power in the hands of the Husbands. If particular care and attention is not paid to the Ladies," Abigail Adams warned, "we are determined to foment a Rebellion, and will not hold ourselves bound by any Laws in which we have no voice, or Representation."

The words of Abigail Adams, one of the earliest American advocates of women's rights, were prophetic. Because when we have not "remembered the ladies," they have, by their words and deeds, reminded us so forcefully of the omission that we cannot fail to remember them. For the history of American women is as interesting and varied as the history of our nation as a whole. American women have played an integral part in founding, settling, and building our country. Some we remember as remarkable women who—against great odds—achieved distinction in the public arena: Anne Hutchinson, who in the 17th century became a charismatic religious leader; Phillis Wheatley, an 18th-century black slave who became a poet; Susan B. Anthony, whose name is synonymous with the 19th-century women's rights movement, and who led the struggle to enfranchise women; and, in our own century, Amelia Earhart, the first woman to cross the Atlantic Ocean by air.

These extraordinary women certainly merit our admiration, but other women, "common women," many of them all but forgotten, should also be recognized for their contributions to American thought and culture. Women have been community builders; they have founded schools and formed voluntary associations to help those in need; they have assumed the major responsibility for rearing children, passing on from one generation to the next the values that keep a culture alive. These and innumerable other contributions, once ignored, are now being recognized by scholars, students, and the public. It is exciting and gratifying to realize that a part of our history that was hardly acknowledged a few generations ago is now being studied and brought to light.

In recent decades, the field of women's history has grown from obscurity to a politically controversial splinter movement to academic respectability, in many cases mainstreamed into such traditional disciplines as history, economics, and psychology. Scholars of women, both female and male, have organized research centers at such prestigious institutions as Wellesley College, Stanford University, and the University of California. Other notable centers for women's studies are the Center for the American Woman and Politics at the Eagleton Institute of Politics at Rutgers University; the Henry A. Murray Research Center for the Study of Lives, at Radcliffe College; and the Women's Research and Education Institute, the research arm of the Congressional Caucus on Women's Issues. Other scholars and public figures have established archives and libraries, such as the Schlesinger Library on the History of Women in America, at Radcliffe College, and the Sophia Smith Collection, at Smith College, to collect and preserve the written and tangible legacies of women.

From the initial donation of the Women's Rights Collection in 1943, the Schlesinger Library grew to encompass vast collections documenting the manifold accomplishments of American women. Simultaneously, the women's movement in general and the academic discipline of women's studies in particular also began with a narrow definition and gradually expanded their mandate. Early causes such as woman suffrage and social reform, abolition and organized labor were joined by newer concerns such as the history of women in business and the professions and in politics and government; the study of the family; and social issues such as health policy and education.

Women, as historian Arthur M. Schlesinger, jr., once pointed out, "have constituted the most spectacular casualty of traditional history. They have made up at least half the human race, but you could never tell that by looking at the books historians write." The new breed of historians is remedying that omission. They have written books about immigrant women and about working-class women who struggled for survival in cities and about black women who met the challenges of life in rural areas. They are telling the stories of women who, despite the barriers of tradition and economics, became lawyers and doctors and public figures.

The women's studies movement has also led scholars to question traditional interpretations of their respective disciplines. For example, the study of war has traditionally been an exercise in military and political analysis, an examination of strategies planned and executed by men. But scholars of women's history have pointed out that wars have also been periods of tremendous change and even opportunity for women, because the very absence of men on the home front enabled them to expand their educational, economic, and professional activities and to assume leadership in their homes.

The early scholars of women's history showed a unique brand of courage in choosing to investigate new subjects and take new approaches to old ones. Often, like their subjects, they endured criticism and even ostracism by their academic colleagues. But their efforts have unquestionably been worthwhile, because with the publication of each new study and book another piece of the historical patchwork is sewn into place, revealing an increasingly comprehensive picture of the role of women in our rich and varied history.

Such books on groups of women are essential, but books that focus on the lives of individuals are equally indispensable. Biographies can be inspirational, offering their readers the example of people with vision who have looked outside themselves for their goals and have often struggled against great obstacles to achieve them. Marian Anderson, for instance, had to overcome racial bigotry in order to perfect her art and perform as a concert singer. Isadora Duncan defied the rules of classical dance to find true artistic freedom. Jane Addams had to break down society's notions of the proper role for women in order to create new social institutions, notably the settlement house. All of these women had to come to terms both with themselves and with the world in which they lived. Only then could they move ahead as pioneers in their chosen callings.

Biography can inspire not only by adulation but also by realism. It helps us to see not only the qualities in others that we hope to emulate, but also, perhaps, the weaknesses that made them "human." By helping us identify with the subject on a more personal level they help us to feel that we, too, can achieve such goals. We read about Eleanor Roosevelt, for instance, who occupied a unique and seemingly enviable position as the wife of the president. Yet we can sympathize with her inner dilemma: an inherently shy woman, she had to force herself to live a most public life in order to use her position to benefit others. We may not be able to imagine ourselves having the immense poetic talent of Emily Dickinson, but from her story we can understand the challenges faced by a creative woman who was expected to fulfill many family responsibilities. And though few of us will ever reach the level of athletic accomplishment displayed by Wilma Rudolph or Babe Zaharias, we can still appreciate their spirit, their overwhelming will to excel.

A biography is a multifaceted lens. It is first of all a magnification, the intimate examination of one particular life. But at the same time, it is a wide-angle lens, informing us about the world in which the subject lived. We come away from reading about one life knowing more about the social, political, and economic fabric of the time. It is for this reason, perhaps, that the great New England essayist Ralph Waldo Emerson wrote, in 1841, "There is properly no history: only biography." And it is also why biography, and particularly women's biography, will continue to fascinate writers and readers alike.

HARRIET BEECHER STOWE

When, in a burst of inspiration, Harriet Beecher Stowe wrote Uncle Tom's Cabin, *she did not know that her book would help change the world.*

ONE

"I Will Write Something"

The station agent surveyed the waiting room of the railroad depot and decided that the ragged family would have to leave. Haggard, unkempt, and overburdened with parcels, they were probably immigrants—in any case, he did not want them in his station. The agent strode toward the group and gruffly told them to wait for their train outside on the platform. Thus, at two o'clock on an April morning in 1850, somewhere in Pennsylvania, Harriet Beecher Stowe rose silently from her seat, gathered up her children and belongings, and stepped out into the chilly night air.

The road-weary Stowe was traveling with three of her five children from Cincinnati, Ohio, to their new home in Brunswick, Maine. The rough journey by train, boat, and stagecoach, endured with little opportunity to rest and even less to bathe, had given the genteel family the appearance of vagabonds. They had little money to pay the rest of their way to Maine, which lay weeks away. Thirty-nine years old and six months pregnant, Stowe had to manage her children and luggage alone. Her troubles, however, had started long before she left Ohio.

The daughter of a respected New England family, Harriet Beecher Stowe had fallen on hard times in Cincinnati. She had lived in the raucous frontier town for nearly 20 years. There, she had married Calvin Stowe, a widely admired but poorly paid professor of religion. During the 14 years since her wedding day, Stowe had struggled to make ends meet while her family grew to include six children. She had used her skills as a writer to supplement the family's income, selling scores of arti-

Stowe and her children traveled part of the way from Ohio to Maine by stagecoach, a slow, uncomfortable mode of transportation.

cles and short stories to magazines and newspapers. Inevitably, the rigors of repeated childbearing and the hard work of running a household had taken their toll on her health. Following the birth of Samuel Charles, her sixth child, she had spent almost a year bedridden with a serious illness. Just as she recovered, her infant son died in a cholera epidemic.

Life in Cincinnati had been all the more disagreeable because of the city's location just over the Ohio River from the slave state of Kentucky. Stowe had glimpsed the horror of slavery through the eyes of blacks who had escaped and made their way across the river. She harbored one particularly vivid memory of a visit she made to a Kentucky plantation, where she had seen slaves toiling in the fields from dawn to dusk. Her opposition to the brutal institution of slavery had grown more passionate with each example of cruelty that she observed or heard about. So, when Calvin Stowe had decided to accept a teaching post at Bowdoin College in Maine, Harriet Beecher Stowe had been more than ready to move far from the slaveholding South.

Stowe had packed the family's possessions and set off with her children, fully expecting to face difficult times in New England: Calvin Stowe would earn a salary of only $1,000 a year at Bowdoin, barely enough to provide for

This portrait of the distinguished Beecher family includes five of seven minister brothers and (seated, left to right) two reformer sisters, their preacher father, a homemaker sister, and the author.

the growing family. Now, as she stood on the dark deserted Pennsylvania train platform, a difficult past behind her and an uncertain future ahead of her, Harriet Beecher Stowe had every reason to feel depressed. But with the passage of each mile eastward her mood had steadily lifted. At long last, she was going home.

When she and her children finally reached New York City, Stowe was in high spirits. She enjoyed a visit with her younger brother, the Reverend Henry Ward Beecher, pastor of the imposing Plymouth Church in Brook-

lyn. Beecher was rapidly becoming one of the most famous preachers in America. Stowe marveled at her brother's success, writing to her husband in Cincinnati of his "beautiful horse and carriage, worth $600." After leaving New York, Stowe traveled to Hartford, Connecticut, to see her sister Mary, and then to Boston, Massachusetts, where she was reunited with her brother Edward, minister of the Park Street Church.

At each stop, Stowe heard talk of the impending Fugitive Slave Act, part of proposed legislation called the Com-

Slaves return from a day of toil in the cotton fields. In Cincinnati, Stowe was daily reminded of slavery's injustice and brutality.

The compromise satisfied Northern and Southern moderates, but one of its elements outraged foes of slavery. If passed, the Fugitive Slave Act would commission federal agents in the free states and territories to track down, capture, and return to bondage escaped slaves. Free states had always been required to return escaped slaves to the South, but until now such action could not be taken without a court hearing. The new law would give federal commissioners absolute control over the delivery of blacks into slavery. If a slaveholder claimed ownership of any black person, that person's future would rest entirely in the hands of an often corrupt and unscrupulous federal agent. "It seemed now," Stowe later wrote, "as if the system [slavery] once confined to the Southern States was rousing itself . . . to extend itself all over the North, and to overgrow the institutions of free society."

Like others opposed to slavery, the Beechers denounced the Fugitive Slave Act, which they felt would make the United States government no better than a slave trader. Ever since they had heard Lyman Beecher, their prominent preacher father, pray for "poor, oppressed, bleeding Africa," the Beecher clan had detested slavery. Now, while Stowe listened, Henry Ward Beecher thundered his disapproval of the prospective law from his pulpit in Brooklyn. At Edward Beecher's dinner table in Boston, Stowe heard her

promise of 1850. In Washington, D.C., Congress had been struggling to resolve the division that had deepened between the Northern and Southern states over the issue of slavery. In the House and the Senate, Southerners anxious to preserve and foster slavery angrily confronted Northerners who sought to limit the expansion of the institution into new territories of the United States. As tensions mounted, Congress devised the Compromise of 1850, an agreement granting concessions to each side in the dispute. Lawmakers hoped the compromise would prevent civil war.

Fugitive Slave Bill.

The Fugitive Slave Act, enacted during the presidency of Millard Fillmore, required "all good citizens" to assist in the recapture of runaway slaves.

Maine on May 22, 1850, "her soul was all on fire with indignation at this new indignity and wrong about to be inflicted by the slave-power on the innocent and defenseless."

Stowe and her children moved into an old house on Federal Street in Brunswick, close by the Bowdoin campus. The big yellow house, pleasant as it was, had been neglected, and Stowe set to work at once. She cleaned, varnished, bought new furniture, and lay carpets. Catharine Beecher joined her sister to help with the housework and with the operation of a small school that the women set up for the local children. In July, Calvin Stowe and the two remaining children arrived from Cincinnati; a week later Harriet Beecher Stowe gave birth to her seventh and last child, Charles Edward.

The household soon settled into a hectic daily routine, which Stowe described in a letter:

Since I began this note I have been called off at least a dozen times; once for the fish man to buy a codfish; once to see a man who brought me some barrels of apples; once to see a book man; then, to Mrs. Upham to see about a drawing I promised to make for her; then to nurse the baby; then into the kitchen to make a chowder for dinner; and now I am at it again, for nothing but deadly determination enables me ever to write. It is rowing against wind and tide.

brother heap scorn on anyone who would cooperate with slaveholders. She quietly took in her brothers' words, adding their ideas to her own already strong convictions. Charles Edward Stowe, her son, reported years later that by the time his mother arrived in

Stowe "rowed against wind and tide" to continue with her writing. Soon, she began publishing pieces in

17

Northerners feared that the Fugitive Slave Act would encourage slave hunts in the free states. The encroachment of the "slave power" outraged them.

the *National Era*, an abolitionist (anti-slavery) journal.

The Fugitive Slave Act was passed that summer, and discussion of it dominated conversation in Brunswick as well as letters Stowe received from her family. Stowe published her own response to the bill, a piece entitled "The Freeman's Dream: A Parable," in August. In the story, she condemns those "who seem to think that there is no standard of right and wrong higher than an act of Congress, or an interpretation of the United States Constitution." The writer found that she could be a voice in the debate over the slavery question.

When, that fall, Stowe received a letter from Edward Beecher's wife, Isabella, an urgent sense of purpose welled up inside her. "Hattie," Isabella Beecher wrote from Boston, "if I could use a pen as you can, I would write something that will make this whole nation feel what an accursed thing slavery is." Stowe read Isabella's letter to her family with such feeling that, as she read it aloud, she rose from her chair, crushed it in her hand, and vowed, "I will write something. I will if I live."

Stowe was determined to join the crusade against slavery, but it would be some time before she could. Her husband had temporarily returned to Cincinnati, and household duties claimed most of her energy. She never forgot her vow, however. In a letter to Calvin Stowe she wrote, "As long as the baby sleeps with me nights I can't do much at anything, but I shall *do it at last*. I shall write that thing if I live. . . ." Much needed encouragement came to town in January 1851, in the midst of a howling blizzard. After completing a speaking engagement in Boston, Henry Ward Beecher made his way through drifts of snow to visit his sister. They talked until dawn about their plans to fight slavery. Stowe, as she later wrote, divulged that she had "begun to do something; I have begun a story, trying to set forth sufferings and wrongs of the slaves." Beecher urged her to go through with it. "Do it, Hattie," he said. "Finish it. . . ."

Beecher's show of enthusiasm and support helped Stowe face the towering challenge of writing about slavery. Even in New England, abolition was not a universally popular cause in 1851. As Stowe put it, "professed abolitionists were a small, despised, unfashionable band." Stowe would risk her reputation, and perhaps even the safety of her family, if she declared her beliefs publicly. In addition, she would face criticism as a woman who dared to speak out on political issues. "Polite" society accepted women writers, but generally limited its approval to those who kept to private subjects such as the family.

With the support of her family, Stowe felt sure she could stand up to any criticism. She was less confident,

In her home on Brunswick's Federal Street, Stowe shouldered her household duties and wondered what she could do about the plight of the slaves.

old black man to death impressed itself upon Stowe's consciousness. She could almost hear the old man praying as he died.

Stowe hurried home, sat down at the small gateleg table in her bedroom, and wrote out the scene that had come to her in church. The next day, because her husband was away, she read what she had written to the only available audience: her sons Henry, 12 years old, and Frederick, age 10. When they heard the story, they broke down sobbing, and one cried, "Oh, mamma! Slavery is the most cruel thing in the world!" When Calvin Stowe returned home, he read the manuscript. He, too, was reduced to tears and begged his wife to write the rest of the story.

"From that time," Harriet Beecher Stowe wrote, "the story can less be said to have been composed by her than imposed upon her. Scenes, incidents, conversations rushed upon her with a vividness and importunity [urgency] that would not be denied." Stowe wrote of her story of slave life to Dr. Gamaliel Bailey, the editor of the *National Era*, asking if he would be interested in publishing a work in several parts. Bailey agreed, offering her $300, which seemed to be a handsome sum for the work.

however, in her ability to write something that would be able to open American eyes to slavery's abominations. Stowe needed a story to tell, but she had no idea where to find it. Then, soon after her brother's visit, inspiration struck.

One Sunday in February 1851, Stowe sat in her pew at the First Parish Church in Brunswick, filled with such emotional turmoil that she hardly heard the sermon. As the minister began the communion ceremony, she seemed to slip into a trance and a "scene presented itself almost as a tangible vision to her mind," according to her own account. The image of a white man forcing two slaves to flog an

Each day, and far into every night, Stowe worked on the story that, in her own words, "was so much more intense a reality to her than any other earthly thing." The first installment

Henry Ward Beecher (holding goblet), Stowe's brother, delivered fiery antislavery sermons and urged his sister to take up her pen for abolition.

appeared in the June 5, 1851, issue of the *National Era*, under the title *UNCLE TOM'S CABIN: or, LIFE AMONG THE LOWLY*. The 3- or 4-part tale Stowe had envisioned expanded to fill 40 weekly installments depicting life and death in the slave states of the South. The response of the public was nothing short of remarkable. Until the last chapter appeared on April 1, 1852, the *National Era* sold out week after week. One reader recounted how "the papers which contained it, after being nearly worn out in going through so many hands...were as carefully folded up and laid away as if the tear stains on them were sacred."

Uncle Tom's Cabin appeared as a book on March 20, 1852. The first edition, 5,000 copies of a 2-volume set bound in cloth and offered at $1.50 each, sold out in 2 days. Within a few months 50,000 had been sold, and by the end of the year 300,000 copies were in circulation in the United States and more than 1.5 million throughout the British Empire. Three power presses ran around the clock and 100 book-

135,000 SETS, 270,000 VOLUMES SOLD.

UNCLE TOM'S CABIN

FOR SALE HERE.

AN EDITION FOR THE MILLION, COMPLETE IN 1 Vol., PRICE 37 1-2 CENTS.
"   "   IN GERMAN, IN 1 Vol., PRICE 50 CENTS.
"   "   IN 2 Vols., CLOTH, 6 PLATES, PRICE $1.50.
SUPERB ILLUSTRATED EDITION, IN 1 Vol., WITH 153 ENGRAVINGS,
PRICES FROM $2.50 TO $5.00.

The Greatest Book of the Age.

An instant sensation, Stowe's novel sold out wherever it appeared. This advertisement lists four separate editions for sale simultaneously.

binders worked feverishly to keep up with the demand. One British journal declared that "the sale of *Uncle Tom's Cabin* is the most marvelous literary phenomenon that the world has ever witnessed."

Stowe's portrait of slavery was the sensation of the day. Through the trials and adventures of her unforgettable characters, she brought to a vast audience a saga of suffering and redemption. Stowe had constructed her tale "to hold up in the most lifelike and graphic manner possible Slavery" because "There is no arguing with *pictures*, and everybody is impressed by them, whether they mean to be or not." Now it seemed as if the whole world had seen her "pictures" and that everyone had an opinion about them. In the North *Uncle Tom's Cabin* roused an outcry against slavery; in the South it produced vehement anger. Harriet Beecher Stowe had written a book that would change the course of history.

While sitting in this church in Brunswick, Maine (shown here in 1850), Stowe saw a vision that inspired her to write Uncle Tom's Cabin.

Harriet Beecher, the 6th of 11 children, grew up in a strictly religious household. She relied on her imagination and her books for amusement.

TWO

"Hattie Is a Genius"

In 1811 Lyman and Roxana Foote Beecher lived on an elm-shaded street in Litchfield, Connecticut. They presided over a household that included five children, an aunt, two or three boarders, several dogs and cats, a horse and a cow, a collection of chickens and pigs, and a hardy corps of rats who had taken up residence under the eaves and behind the wallboard. The house was bursting at the seams, but on June 14, 1811, another tenant, a little girl named Harriet Elizabeth, arrived. On hearing of his daughter's birth Lyman Beecher remarked, "wish it had been a boy."

In 1813, a little brother, Henry Ward, was born, and he and Harriet soon became inseparable. They did everything together, including get into mischief. Once, they crawled into a closet where they found a sack of tulip bulbs, which they mistook for onions and promptly ate. They escaped punishment, probably because the stunt amused their mother.

Harriet and her brother would never really know their forgiving mother. Roxana Foote Beecher died of tuberculosis in 1816, when Harriet was only five years old. "The angelic mother whom I scarcely knew in the world ... has been to me only a spiritual presence through life," Harriet later wrote. By contrast, Lyman Beecher would exert tremendous influence on his daughter's life for years to come. The son of a blacksmith, he was born in 1775, when Puritanism was still a powerful force in American religion. Beecher attended Yale College, where he studied the stern Calvinist theology of Jonathan Edwards, a fiery revivalist preacher. A Puritan of the old school, Beecher be-

Harriet was born in this house in Litchfield, Connecticut, where her father was the minister of a Congregational church.

lieved that people's "immortal souls are sleeping on the brink of hell" and could not be saved from eternal torment except by undergoing a spiritual conversion and submitting to the will of God.

By the time of Harriet's birth, Beecher was well on his way to becoming one of the nation's most eminent Congregationalist preachers. Among other things, he was renowned far and wide as a crusader against strong drink. He delivered sermons condemning the use of "ardent spirits" (alcoholic beverages) and, in an age when rum mixed with opium served as a common remedy for childhood illnesses, he begged parents to keep alcohol from their

homes. Printed copies of his sermons were distributed throughout New England, winning an enthusiastic response and spurring a nationwide temperance campaign. Beecher also advocated other social reforms, including the abolition of dancing, dueling, and Sunday mail delivery.

To Harriet, Lyman Beecher seemed "the image of the Heavenly Father" and her home "a kind of moral heaven." Conversations around the kitchen table often took the form of theological debates. Harriet listened to, but as a girl rarely took part in, these discussions, which her father used to teach her brothers his philosophy. By training them to argue, Beecher encouraged his children to think for themselves. He admonished them to "let no creed bind you because it is reputed orthodox," but he made it clear that their "independent" thinking should bring them to his own point of view. He warned them not to accept any argument "until you perceive its agreement with the Scriptures"—as Lyman Beecher interpreted them.

Harriet's father did have a gentle side, which came out when he played his violin and roughhoused with the children. Lyman Beecher was a man of enormous physical energy whom his children found easy to love. Outside the house in Litchfield, he built himself a set of exercise rings and parallel bars and swung about while the neighbors

Roxana Foote Beecher died when Harriet was only five years old. As a result, Harriet's father would be the main influence on her life.

life, his seemingly endless talk of sin and salvation often made life at the Beechers' gloomy. He never allowed Harriet and her siblings to forget his conviction that their souls would be damned unless they converted. Not surprisingly, Harriet spent some of her happiest moments away from her father. Soon after her mother's death she traveled to Nutplains, Connecticut, to stay with her mother's family. The Footes were Episcopalians who took a more liberal view of morality than did Lyman Beecher. Grandmother Foote indulged Harriet, seldom scolded her, and introduced her to poetry. Years later, Harriet described her grandmother's house as a "paradise. . . . To us, every juniper bush, every wild sweetbrier, every barren, sandy hillside, every stony pasture, spoke of bright hours of love."

In 1817, a year after Roxana's death, Lyman Beecher married Harriet Porter, a young woman from Portland, Maine. The new Mrs. Beecher took to Harriet at once, describing her as "amiable, affectionate, and very bright." The Beecher children accepted their father's new wife but never developed any real warmth for her. Harriet Porter Beecher, "a lady of great personal elegance" according to her stepdaughter, found the life of a poor minister's wife difficult. She bore 4 children, bringing the household total to 11, and tried to manage on her husband's $800 a year. It soon became obvious, Harriet later

watched in amazement. He also kept a huge pile of sand in the basement so that during periods of bad weather he could grab a shovel and dig in for a workout. Beecher fished and hunted with equal fervor, rushing from the house whenever he saw a flock of birds and blasting away at them with his shotgun.

Although Lyman Beecher tempered his Puritanism with an enthusiasm for

Lyman Beecher preached against the "demon rum," which he and other temperance crusaders blamed for a host of physical and social ills.

reported, that "her nature and habits were too refined and exacting for the bringing up of chidren of great animal force and vigor, under the strain and pressure of straitened [deprived] circumstances." Harriet's older sister Mary would shortly write: "Mamma is not well, and don't laugh any more that she used to."

By this time, Harriet could read fluently and spent hours in her father's study poring over his books. Lyman Beecher recognized his daughter's superior mind and wrote when she was only eight that "Hattie is a genius. I would give a hundred dollars if she was a boy." He enrolled his "genius" at Miss Sarah Pierce's school in Litchfield, where Harriet excelled in her studies. At 12 she wrote an essay entitled, "Can the Immortality of the Soul

Be Proved by the Light of Nature?" and a teacher read it to a large audience crowded into the town hall for the school's annual exhibition. Lyman Beecher listened with interest and asked the teacher who had written it. Harriet beamed as he learned that she was the author. "To have interested him was past all juvenile triumphs," she said years later.

Although proud of Harriet's abilities, Lyman Beecher worried that his daughter's active imagination might interfere with her spiritual development. "She is as odd as she is intelligent and studious," he wrote, and warned her that she "must break up the habit" of daydreaming "or be damned." But Harriet could not give up her books. She learned the stories of *The Arabian Nights* by heart and one summer read Sir Walter Scott's *Ivanhoe* seven times.

More than anything else she encountered, though, Harriet loved the romantic poetry of Lord Byron. When she read *The Corsair*, she wrote that she felt "astonished and electrified." Lord Byron's death in 1824 left her despondent. Upon hearing the news of his passing, she climbed a hill behind the house in Litchfield and "lay down among the daisies looking up into the blue sky, and thought of that great eternity into which Byron had entered, and wondered how it might be with his soul."

That summer, when she was 13,

Harriet also worried "how it might be" with her own soul. She had listened for years to Lyman Beecher's sermons, which spoke to her of the need for complete submission to God. Yet she could not find within herself an absolute willingness to sacrifice everything for the stern God she had been taught to believe in. Then, one Sunday, she heard her father speak of Christ as a patient friend. "Oh! how much I needed just such a friend," she thought and decided to commit herself to God. Her conversion, however, was short-lived. When asked, "Do you feel that if the universe should be destroyed, you could be happy with God alone?" Harriet hesitated. She realized that she could not answer with an unqualified "yes." At that moment, she understood that she would never be the Christian her father expected her to be.

Spiritual doubts would trouble Harriet into adulthood, when she would finally reach her own conclusions regarding religion. As an adolescent, she expressed despair in letters to her brother Edward: "My whole life is one continued struggle. I do nothing right. I yield to temptation almost as soon as it assails me. . . . My sins take away all my happiness." Harriet's sister Catharine, 11 years her senior, knew what it was like to suffer under Lyman Beecher's unyielding religious system. When her fiancé had drowned at sea several years earlier, her father had

Harriet's father, a charismatic, iron-willed man, dominated the Beecher household and had a lasting influence on the lives of all his children.

offered no comfort. Instead, he had asserted that the young man's unconverted soul had no doubt been damned to hell. Catharine Beecher from that point on rejected her father's religion and devoted her energy to other pursuits. Now she took Harriet under her wing.

In 1823, Catharine Beecher, who would become a major reformer in the area of education for women, estab-

Genteel stepmother Harriet Porter (shown here with her daughter Isabella Beecher) never adapted to life with the rustic Beecher family.

The poetry of Lord Byron enthralled Harriet Beecher and provided her an escape from the strains of a harshly puritanical and often dreary home life.

lished the Hartford Female Academy, a school for young women. She invited Harriet to enroll, and in the fall of 1824 Harriet packed her few belongings in a carpetbag and traveled the 30 miles from Litchfield to Hartford, Connecticut. Harriet moved in with a family who were friends of her father and tried to adjust to life in the bustling city of 6,000. She studied writing, arithmetic, Italian, and French, as well as Latin, which she taught herself from a textbook. Still, she found time for herself and began writing *Cleon*, a drama in verse heavily influenced by the work of her idol, Lord Byron. When Cath-

arine Beecher discovered Harriet's secret project, she made sure her little sister would have no more time for such unseemly pursuits by setting her to work studying a difficult theological tract. By the time Harriet turned 14, she was teaching the material to students her own age.

In 1826, Lyman Beecher accepted a position at the Hanover Street Church in Boston, Massachusetts. He withdrew Harriet from school in Hartford and brought her with the rest of the family to Boston, where she enrolled in a day school. At first Harriet was fascinated by the historic sites surrounding her. "Within a stone's throw of our door," she recalled, "was the old Cop Hill burying ground where rested the bones of the Puritan fathers." Harriet also watched with interest while her father pursued his many moral campaigns.

But at the age of 15 she had other concerns, chief among them a serious state of depression. She wrote to Catharine that their stepmother "often tells me that I am a strange, inconsistent being. Sometimes I could not sleep and have groaned and cried till midnight, while in the daytime I tried to appear cheerful and succeeded so well that Papa reproved me for laughing so much." Henry Ward Beecher described his melancholy sister as "owling about." In her dark moods Harriet was capable of bleak sentiment. "I wish I could die young," she wrote Catharine, "and let the remembrance of me and my faults perish in the grave, rather than live, a trouble to everyone. How perfectly wretched I often feel—so useless, so weak, so destitute of all energy."

Catharine persuaded Lyman Beecher to send Harriet back to Hartford. "Harriet will have young society here all the time," she explained, "and I think cheerful and amusing friends will do much for her." She also revealed another motive for bringing Harriet back to her school: "I can do better in preparing her to teach . . . than anyone else, for I know best what is needed." When Harriet returned to

Catharine Beecher founded the Hartford Female Academy in 1823. Harriet studied and taught at her sister's school until her departure for Ohio in 1832.

Hartford in 1827, Catharine's thriving school, now called the Hartford Female Seminary, enrolled more than a hundred students and occupied an impressive new building of its own. Harriet continued her studies and began teaching a Latin class. In her free time she developed her talent as an artist, drawing, sketching, and painting in both oil and watercolor. She wrote that she often worked "from nine in the morning till after dark at night."

Only 16 years old, Harriet soon became a full-time teacher, instructing students in English composition, rhetoric, and art. Life settled into an agreeable routine of morning horseback rides, teaching, drawing and painting, letter writing, and summertime visits to her family in Boston. This routine might well have become permanent,

Harriet enjoyed "a world of love" in Hartford, where she often took strolls along the riverfront with her two close friends, Georgiana May and Mary Dutton.

for teaching was one of the few careers open to an unmarried 19th-century woman of Harriet Beecher's class, and Harriet showed not the slightest sign of getting married. More interested in books than boyfriends, the shy young woman never mentioned a single suitor in all her long letters to family and friends.

Harriet did, however, enjoy the company of two close friends. With Georgiana May, the first friend she made in Hartford, Harriet took long walks by the banks of the Park River and confided her hopes and fears. Georgiana helped Harriet escape the despair that had overwhelmed her in Boston, and finally Harriet could write to Georgiana that "I have come to a firm resolution to count no hours but unclouded ones and let all others slip out of my memory as quickly as possible." In her friendship with Georgiana, which she called "a heaven—a world of love," Harriet rediscovered life's charms, noting that "love after all is the lifeblood, the existence, the all in all of mind."

Harriet roomed with her other friend, Mary Dutton, who taught mathematics at Catharine's school. The two teachers gossiped about their students, joked about Harriet's serious sister, and wondered about the future. In an 1830 letter to Mary, Harriet revealed that she was trying to learn as much about writing as she could: "I am quite busy preparing for my composition class," she reported. "Have been reading Rasselas & writing a little in imitation of Dr. Johnson's style— think it is improving me by giving me a command of language." At the age of 18, Harriet Beecher had already taken the first steps toward becoming one of the most powerful voices of her time.

That year, Lyman Beecher's Boston church caught fire and burned to the ground. The city's fire fighters, who disliked Beecher for his strident crusade against alcohol, made no effort to extinguish the flames. Hundreds of onlookers watched in astonishment as jugs of rum stored in the basement exploded in the heat. Unbeknownst to Beecher, a liquor merchant had rented storage space in the church. Jokes about "Beecher's broken jugs" circulated throughout the city, which had wearied of the preacher's devotion to a variety of unpopular causes. When Beecher tried to raise funds to rebuild the church, he got little support.

Beecher began to look west for opportunity. In the 1830s the rich, plentiful land of the American West—then the Ohio River Valley, which included Indiana, Illinois, Ohio, and Kentucky—attracted thousands of new settlers each year. Beecher felt that he had a duty to bring his message to the frontier. "If we gain the west all is safe," he said, "if we lose it, all is lost." In 1832, he answered a call to be president of Lane Seminary in Cincinnati, Ohio. Ten Beechers, including Harriet and Catharine, set out that October for "The Queen City."

When his Boston church burned, Lyman Beecher could not raise funds to rebuild it. He decided to go west and direct the Lane Seminary in Cincinnati, Ohio.

In Cincinnati, Harriet Beecher met and married Calvin Stowe, a professor at Lane Seminary. Life with the respected theologian would be financially unstable.

THREE

"What Is There to Be Done?"

"**I** never saw a place so capable of being rendered a Paradise," wrote Catharine Beecher of Cincinnati. For her part, Harriet Beecher liked Cincinnati well enough—at first. She might have agreed with the words of English novelist Charles Dickens, who said, "I have not often seen a place that commends itself so favorably to the stranger at first glance." Set on a group of hills along the north bank of the Ohio River, the booming western metropolis of 30,000 abounded with lovely homes and stately commercial buildings. Cincinnati also boasted fine schools, several literary societies, talented musical groups, and lively theaters, but close examination revealed a much less attractive town.

Many referred to the river port as "Porkopolis" because of the aromatic complex of slaughterhouses and meat-packing plants that operated by the river. Pigs roamed the garbage-strewn streets foraging for food, and frequent cholera epidemics ravaged the hot, unsanitary town. Harriet Beecher summed up her opinion of the situation when she saw her four-year-old half brother playing with a hog. "Very disgusting," she wrote.

More disturbing than the presence of the pork industry was the proximity of an evil institution flourishing just across the river in Kentucky: slavery. In New England, slavery had seemed a distant, even abstract, problem, but in Ohio it was an everyday reality. Cincinnati had close economic ties with the neighboring South and thus indirectly

Some observers dubbed Cincinnati, a cosmopolitan city, "The Athens of the West," but others referred to the dirty frontier town as "Porkopolis."

relied on the slave trade. Beecher could read shocking newspaper advertisements that offered generous rewards for the return of slaves who had escaped to freedom in Ohio. She could see escaped slaves and hear their stories. And all around her raged battles between the various factions in the slavery debate.

Leaving that struggle to others for the time being, Harriet Beecher settled with her family into a house next door to Lane Seminary. The school, located outside the city in Walnut Hills, had one teacher and three students when the Beechers arrived, but Lyman Beecher had big plans for the place. He had raised funds for the seminary at numerous stops on the family's jour-

ney west, and when he arrived in Cincinnati on November 14, 1832, he enthusiastically took up the challenge of developing the school.

While their father assumed his duties there, Catharine and Harriet Beecher resumed teaching, in a new school Catharine opened for girls. Harriet's work at the Western Female Institute left her little time for herself. She wrote to her friend Georgiana May, "My whole time has been taken up with the labor of our new school, or wasted in the fatigue and lassitude following such labor." Serving as her elder sister's loyal assistant, Beecher rose before dawn six days a week to teach classes and help manage the school. The sisters also published a

Under Lyman Beecher's direction, Lane Seminary expanded rapidly, but a rebellion of abolitionist students soon reversed the school's fortunes.

geography textbook, written by the younger but credited to both of them. And the budding writer began placing pieces in local magazines and newspapers, the first appearing in June 1833.

That year Beecher had her first—and only—glimpse of slavery in action when she and her friend Mary Dutton visited the Kentucky plantation of a student's family. There they stayed in an elegant house with broad verandas surrounded by smooth lawns of Kentucky bluegrass. During the days they watched slaves tilling fields of corn, hemp, and tobacco and examined the rough, vine-covered log cabins where the slaves lived. In the evenings, they feasted on lavish offerings of duck, chicken, turkey, and ham. Afterwards,

they sat in the drawing room while the plantation owner ordered slaves to sing and dance as entertainment for his guests. On one of these evenings, Beecher and Dutton met a young woman with skin only slightly darker than theirs. She was the child of a black woman and a white man, but a slave nonetheless. Beecher quietly observed every detail and committed it to memory before returning to Cincinnati.

In Cincinnati, Beecher spent most of her time in the company of her family and Lane Seminary's faculty and students. Leading such a protected life, she never developed the "social graces." An acquaintance recalled that she was "inattentive to what we had

When Harriet Beecher visited Kentucky in 1833, she witnessed slavery firsthand. Nearly 20 years later, she would record her observations in Uncle Tom's Cabin.

been sedulously [carefully] taught as 'the Minor Morals' ''—the rules of fashionable dress and demeanor. Still, according to the same young man, though "rather careless of dress & manner & absent minded," Beecher was "feminine, kind, & with a quick apprehension [sense] of humor, which pleased us very much." In August 1833 Beecher met two other people who appreciated her qualities: Professor Calvin Stowe, a stocky theologian in his early thirties, and his wife Eliza Tyler Stowe.

Harriet Beecher liked Professor Stowe, but was at first more interested in Eliza Stowe. "I fell in love with her directly," she wrote of her pretty, refined new friend. The two women shared many interests, attending the meetings of local literary societies and discussing the exciting recent events at Lane Seminary. A growing number of the students there were active abolitionists agitating for the immediate emancipation of all slaves. Led by Theodore Weld, who would become one of the nation's most prominent antislavery crusaders, the students had established an organization to educate local blacks, and some even dared to socialize with the residents of Cincinnati's so-called "Little Africa." Their activities had offended and enraged the city's proslavery whites, and Lane increasingly came under attack as a bastion of the hated abolitionist movement.

President Lyman Beecher implored the students to be more cautious, both because of the potential for violence and because he feared dismissal by the school's conservative board of trustees. He also disagreed with the abolitionists' radical stance, taking the position that slavery should be abolished at some distant point in the future when everyone agreed that it was no longer workable. Thus, in August 1834, when Lane Seminary's trustees passed a ruling that prohibited all student discussion of slavery—even in private—and their attempts to help local blacks, Lyman Beecher decided to enforce it. Protesting that the administration was trying to outlaw the constitutionally guaranteed freedoms of speech and association, 40 students—most of the student body—resigned. Lyman Beecher and the trustees realized their error and reversed the ruling, but none of the students returned. Its reputation and prosperity ruined, Lane Seminary would never recover.

Tragedy struck the Stowe household at the same time. After only a year in Ohio, Calvin Stowe wrote of his wife that life in the West had "laid her loveliness in ruins." When cholera swept through the city in the summer of 1834, the epidemic claimed the life of Harriet Beecher's best friend. Eliza

Theodore Weld led the uprising of abolitionist students at Lane Seminary. He later became one of slavery's most prominent assailants.

Stowe's death crushed Harriet Beecher and left Calvin Stowe virtually helpless. Although a brilliant and respected scholar of the Bible, Stowe had little skill in dealing with the practical matters of life. The Beechers helped see him through the dark days following his wife's death; Harriet was the most attentive because she shared his grief. As Stowe regained his good cheer, he turned his attention to Harriet Beecher. The two spent more and more time together, and slowly they fell in love.

In many ways, Harriet Beecher and

Calvin Stowe made a perfect match. She came from a family of preachers; he was a clergyman. Both were natives of New England; Stowe amused Beecher for hours with his seemingly endless stock of colorful stories about Massachusetts, his home state. Beecher possessed a keen intellect and admired learning in others; Stowe was a renowned thinker. When Stowe spoke one evening at the Semi-Colon Club, a local literary society, Beecher wrote, "If ever a woman feels proud of her lover it is when she sees him as a successful public speaker." She found that she could close her eyes to Stowe's faults—his financial incompetence, his gluttony, his indecisiveness, and his hypochondria. Beecher decided it was time to marry, and Professor Stowe seemed a good choice. Late in 1835 they were engaged.

On January 6, 1836, Lyman Beecher married his daughter Harriet Beecher, age 25, to Calvin Stowe, age 34. Just before her wedding, the bride wrote nervously to her friend Georgiana May:

> Well, my dear G., about half an hour more and your old friend, companion, schoolmate, sister, etc., will cease to be Hatty Beecher and change to nobody knows who.... I have been dreading and dreading the time, and lying awake all last week wondering how I should live through this overwhelming crisis, and lo! it has come, and I feel *nothing at all.*

Nevertheless, once the "overwhelming crisis" had come to pass,

Opposed to slavery but favoring a cautious, moderate approach to the problem, Lyman Beecher did not support the activities of his radical students.

Harriet Beecher Stowe wrote to Georgiana May, "I am tranquil, quiet, and happy."

A few months after the wedding Calvin Stowe left for an extended trip to Europe, where he was to purchase books for Lane Seminary's library and study the German school system for the state of Ohio. Harriet Beecher Stowe had planned to travel east to see him off from New York, but the discovery that she was pregnant canceled her plans. Wistfully, she wrote her husband as he prepared to sail: "My dear, I wish I were a man in your place;

if I wouldn't have a grand time!" She moved in with her family, resumed writing short articles for the *Western Monthly Magazine* and the Cincinnati *Journal and Western Luminary*, and awaited the birth of her child.

The summer of 1836 brought violence to the streets of Cincinnati and new understanding to the mind of Harriet Beecher Stowe. Abolitionist James G. Birney had published the first issue of his Cincinnati-based antislavery newspaper, the *Philanthropist*, early that year. Each subsequent issue had aroused increasing anger among the city's large proslavery population, and in July the rage erupted into fighting. A mob broke into the paper's offices and damaged Birney's press. Stowe wrote to her husband that "the mob madness is certainly upon this city.... Already my sympathies are strongly enlisted for Mr. Birney, and I hope that he will stand his ground and assert his rights." She felt so strongly that she published a moderate but nonetheless daring article defending Birney's right to free speech.

A few days later the mob dumped Birney's press into the Ohio River and swarmed through the streets in search of the publisher. They wreaked havoc in the city's black neighborhood, then, led by the mayor, scoured a hotel in hopes of finding Birney. The abolitionist escaped, but the incident had shocked Stowe into a new awareness of the evils of slavery. Years later she

A supporter of slavery threatens an abolitionist. The proslavery violence sweeping through Cincinnati alerted Stowe to "the real nature of slavery."

told her son Charles that "I saw for the first time clearly that the institution of slavery was incapable of defence, and that it was for that reason that its supporters were compelled to mob-violence.... That summer and fall opened my eyes to the real nature of slavery as they had never been opened before."

Stowe (left) came to share the immediate emancipation view of Henry Ward Beecher (seated), rejecting the conservative position of Catharine Beecher (right).

On September 29, 1836, Harriet Beecher Stowe gave birth to twin girls and named them Eliza Tyler Stowe, after Calvin's first wife, and Isabella Beecher Stowe. Calvin returned from Europe in January 1837 and promptly insisted that Isabella's name be changed to honor his second wife, and so the baby became Harriet Beecher Stowe. The growing family moved into their own house in Walnut Hills and hired a housekeeper, a young black woman.

Not long afterward, the Stowes discovered that their maid, who claimed to be legally free, was in fact a runaway slave whose master was in Cincinnati hunting for her. Calvin Stowe and his brother-in-law Henry Ward Beecher armed themselves with pistols and in the middle of the night smuggled the fugitive out of the city by wagon. They took her to a farm that served as a stop on the Underground Railroad—the network of abolitionists who helped escaped slaves make their way north to freedom. The crisis left Harriet Beecher Stowe more upset about slavery than ever. She asked her husband, "Pray, what is there in Cincinnati to satisfy one whose mind is awakened on this subject? No one can have the system of slavery brought before him without an irrepressible desire to *do* something, and what is there to be done?"

Other members of the Beecher family had been asking the same question. Lyman and Catharine Beecher maintained a conservative position, advocating gradual abolition and "colonization," the return of black Americans to African soil. Brothers William and Henry Ward Beecher were gradually adopting the immediate emancipation stance already taken by two other Beecher brothers, George and Edward. Edward Beecher, an active crusader for abolition, preached and wrote against slavery and had already lost a good friend to the bullets of a proslavery mob. With each passing day, Stowe and her husband felt increasing sympathy for radical abolitionists such as Edward Beecher.

Household concerns, however, dominated Stowe's attention. In January 1838 she gave birth to a little boy whom she named Henry, and her duties became even more burdensome. "I am a mere drudge with few ideas beyond babies and housekeeping," Stowe wrote. Waking each day before sunrise, "I get my frock half on and baby by that time has kicked himself down off his pillow, and is crying." Then came nursing, cooking, dusting, washing, and ironing, all while Stowe listened to the twins "chattering, hallowing, or singing at the tops of their voices." The strain wore on her, and her depression returned. Upon paying a visit to her sister, Catharine Beecher found Stowe "not so well as to nerves.... I hope she is to have an interval of rest."

But there would be no rest for the

Edward Beecher was the first of the family to adopt a radical antislavery stance. A proslavery mob murdered his friend Elijah Lovejoy, an abolitionist.

young wife and mother. In May 1840 son Frederick William arrived. The difficult pregnancy and delivery left Stowe bedridden; for a year she struggled to regain her health. An even more persistent enemy than illness, though, was the poverty that plagued the household. Since the 1834 uprising, Lane Seminary had teetered on the edge of financial ruin. Calvin Stowe earned a teaching salary of only $600 a

year and seemed incapable of finding other support for his family.

As debts mounted, Harriet Beecher Stowe shouldered more and more of the financial burden herself. She found time to write nearly every day and published her work frequently. "If you see my name coming out everywhere," Stowe wrote to Mary Dutton, "you can be sure of one thing—that I do it for the pay. I have determined not to be a mere domestic slave." Stowe used part of her earnings to hire a housekeeper, so that she would have more time to write. Publishers gladly paid $1.50 or $2.00 per page for her stories of family life in New England.

Although Stowe met with success in the literary world, her life remained hard. The winter of 1842 was, in her words, "a season of sickness and gloom," during which typhoid fever struck Cincinnati. In 1843 Stowe's elder brother George Beecher shot and killed himself, perhaps intentionally, leaving the entire Beecher clan morose. When, that August, Stowe gave birth to her fifth child, a daughter named Georgiana May, her health crumbled, confining her to bed for months. The baby was weak and barely clung to life. Stowe wrote that she felt "haunted and pursued by care that seemed to drink my life blood."

Stowe found some respite from domestic cares in writing, and in the hard year of 1843 publication of her first book brightened her economic prospects. Harper and Brothers, a New York publisher, printed a collection of her magazine stories under the title *The Mayflower: Sketches of Scenes and Characters among the Descendants of the Pilgrims*. She earned only a small royalty, but wrote to her husband, "On the whole, my dear, if I choose to be a literary lady, I have, I think, as good a chance of making a profit by it as any one I know of."

Calvin Stowe responded to his wife's success with enthusiasm: "My dear, you must be a literary woman. It is so written in the book of fate." He advised her to "Write [sign] yourself fully and always Harriet Beecher Stowe, which is a name euphonious [pleasant sounding], flowing, and full of meaning. Then, my word for it, your husband will lift up his head in the gate, and your children will rise up and call you blessed."

Full of encouragement as he was, Calvin Stowe offered his wife little practical assistance in running the household. He was frequently away from home, leaving her to cope on her own. When home, he often took to his bed and complained loudly if life's troubles overwhelmed him. Hallucinatory phantoms inhabited his inner world, distracting him from his responsibilities as a scholar, husband, and father. He imagined himself the victim of every possible physical ailment. His wife, meanwhile, suffered from painfully real headaches and eye

Often overwhelmed by the demands placed on women of her class, Harriet Beecher Stowe termed the struggle to fulfill her duties "a daily death."

Cholera, spread via contaminated food, was a common cause of death in the 19th century. In 1849 it claimed Stowe's infant son Samuel Charles.

trouble. On more days than not, Harriet Beecher Stowe slipped into a black mood. "It is a dark, sloppy, rainy, muddy, disagreeable day," she wrote in June 1845, "and I have been working hard (for me) all day. . . . I am sick of the smell of sour milk, and sour meat, and sour everything . . . everything smells mouldy; and altogether I feel as if I never wanted to eat again."

In March 1846 Stowe sought some relief, traveling to a spa in Vermont to take a water cure, a regimen of special showers and baths then believed to remedy all kinds of ailments. She returned to Cincinnati in the spring of 1847, and in January 1848, at the age of 37, she gave birth to her sixth child, a son named Samuel Charles. In June Calvin Stowe left for his own stint at the spa and stayed away for more than a year. In his absence, calamity descended upon the household.

The summer of 1849 brought the worst cholera epidemic yet to Cincinnati. Thousands died, and as hearses rumbled through the streets, infant Samuel Charles went into convulsions. Stowe wrote to her husband, "We have been watching all day by the dying bed of little Charley, who is gradually sinking. There is no hope now of his surviving the night." The baby died the next day and Stowe wrote, "At last it is over, and our dear little one is gone from us." Even in her grief, though, she observed the suffering of those around her. "I write as though there were no sorrow like my sorrow," she reflected, "yet there has been in this city, as in the land of Egypt, scarce a house without its dead."

Harriet Beecher Stowe would soon leave "the land of Egypt"—the land of her exile—and return home to her beloved New England.

This lithograph depicts scenes of slavery. Through Uncle Tom's Cabin, *Stowe sought to open American eyes to the horrors of life in bondage.*

FOUR

Uncle Tom's Cabin

When Harriet Beecher Stowe arrived in Maine in 1850, most Northerners had just begun to consider the slavery question. "Our feeling in the North till that time," according to prominent New Yorker George Templeton Strong, had been "not hostility to slavery, but indifference to it, and reluctance to discuss it. It was a disagreeable subject with which we had nothing to do." But when the Fugitive Slave Act made the Northern states accountable for runaway slaves, "it made slavery visible in our communities." Opposition to slavery grew rapidly in the free states, soon fed further by "a sentimental romance, *Uncle Tom's Cabin*," that set Northerners "crying and sobbing over the sorrows" of enslaved blacks.

Uncle Tom's Cabin related a tale of abuse and suffering that had waited too long to be told. When Swedish novelist Frederika Bremer traveled through the United States in 1850, she could not help wondering why so little had been written about slavery. "I know of no subject," she wrote, "which could furnish opportunities for more heart-rending or more picturesque descriptions or scenes.... I cannot understand why, in particular, noble-minded...American mothers who have hearts and genius do not take up the subject and treat it with a power which should pierce through bone and marrow...."

Harriet Beecher Stowe's *Uncle Tom's Cabin*, published in 1852, pierced the "bone and marrow" of an already bleeding nation. Slavery had been a troublesome feature of North American life ever since Dutch merchants first brought slaves to Jamestown, Virginia, in 1619. (The Portuguese had established the institution in the Carribean and South America before 1500.) Before the transatlantic slave trade ended, European traders imported more than 9 million kidnapped Africans to the New World to satisfy the demand for laborers to work on large plantations growing tobacco, rice, and cotton. By 1850, 3.2 million slaves toiled on plantations in the southern United States. By the time the Civil War started in 1861, that number would rise to more than 4 million.

Until the Thirteenth Amendment outlawed slavery in 1865, most American blacks lived in bondage on plantations of 50 to 100 slaves. Three-quarters of the slave population worked on cotton plantations. Planters generally provided their slaves with the barest necessities of life—small crude cabins, one or two sets of clothing, and a bit of cornmeal and salt pork—and nothing more. Slaves worked from dawn to dusk six days a week, sometimes longer. The threat of the whip and other, harsher means of punishment darkened every day of slave life, and black women suffered frequent rape at the hands of their white masters. Fully one-third of all slave families were torn apart by the sale of members to different owners. Even when lenient masters softened these harsh realities, slaves could never forget that the law denied them every human right and freedom.

Slavery had not developed in the United States without opposition. Even before winning independence from Britain, American colonists made some attempts to regulate the growth of the institution. In 1726, colonists in Virginia unsuccessfully petitioned the British government to block the importation of slaves from abroad. Quakers took up the abolitionist cause in 1760, sparking the American antislavery movement, which grew to include approximately 140 organizations by 1827. Freed and escaped blacks represented a large proportion of abolitionists, and slaves, too, rose to their own defense, rebelling sporadically throughout the South.

The most famous of the slave uprisings occured in 1831, when Nat Turner and five fellow slaves killed their master and spread the insurrection to nearby plantations in Southampton County, Virginia. Some 70 slaves revolted, killing 57 whites, before government forces intervened and arrested Turner and his compatriots. Turner was tried and executed. Southerners responded to the Turner rebellion by passing laws that made life even more difficult for slaves. Their action provoked Northern abolitionists, who hardened their stance against slavery and accelerated their efforts to end it. By 1838 approximately 1,350 antislavery societies with a total membership of 250,000 worked to abolish the South's "peculiar institution." These groups published periodicals, rallied popular antislavery sentiment, and pushed for legislative reforms.

Abolitionists also helped runaway slaves make their way north to freedom via the Underground Railroad. An estimated total of 60,000 to 75,000 slaves fled along this network of safe houses and secret routes. Some escaped slaves, such as Frederick Douglass, who published three autobiographies describing his days in bondage, worked unflaggingly to free American blacks. Sojourner Truth, freed legally, was another former slave who spurred antislavery activity. She traveled throughout the North speaking out against the horrors of slavery and in 1850 published *The Narrative of Sojourner Truth*, the story of her life as a slave.

As they learned more about conditions in the South, abolitionists of the 1830s and 1840s adopted an increasingly radical position on slavery, turning away from the notion that slavery could end gradually and American blacks could be "colonized," or returned to Africa. But the rise of "immediatism"—the movement for the immediate emancipation of all slaves and the integration of freed blacks into American society—alarmed many Northerners as well as Southerners. Those who had not joined the crusade against slavery often blamed the antislavery activists for stirring up trouble. Mob violence directed against abolitionists erupted with increasing fre-

North America's first slaves arrive in Jamestown, Virginia, in 1619. For nearly 250 years, slavery blighted the British colonies that became the United States.

quency, while in Congress Southerners fought Northerners over the future of slavery.

Congress attempted to heal the sectional rift with the Compromise of 1850, which included the Fugitive Slave Act. The effort backfired by arousing the indignation of Northerners, who were now expected to cooperate with the South in the perpetuation of slavery. One of those outraged by the new

Slaves harvest cotton in the American South. Slaveholders forced blacks of all ages to perform such backbreaking tasks from dawn to dusk, six days a week.

law was Harriet Beecher Stowe. She published a number of articles in Dr. Gamaliel Bailey's antislavery journal, the *National Era*, and then decided "to write some sketches which should show to the world slavery as she had herself seen it." Because she felt that few Northerners would believe her tale if she presented slavery at its cruelest, she set out to "show the *best side* of

A government agent arrests Nat Turner, the slave who led an 1831 revolt in Virginia. The rebellion resulted in the deaths of 57 whites; Turner was executed.

the thing, and something *faintly approaching the worst.*" In addition, she wrote, "It was her object to show that the evils of slavery were the inherent evils of a bad *system*, and not always the fault of those who had become involved in it."

As she set out to write *Uncle Tom's Cabin*, Stowe drew on her own observations, supplemented by background research and a vivid imagination, to create a detailed exposé of slavery. During her 18 years in Cincinnati she had seen slave traders and slave hunters at work and had helped fugitive slaves evade them. Her 1833 trip to Kentucky had given her a firsthand glimpse of slavery, and she had read autobiographical accounts of slavery by Frederick Douglass and others. She had listened to stories told her by former slaves, heard antislavery workers debate the issues, and read scores of newspaper articles about slavery and the abolition movement. She had also observed the operation of Cincinnati's active Underground Railroad and had witnessed violent confrontations between proslavery and antislavery factions. All of this experience went into *Uncle Tom's Cabin*.

Uncle Tom's Cabin traces the lives of Tom, a pious Christian slave, and George and Eliza Harris and their small son Harry, also slaves. When the story opens, Tom, Eliza, and Harry live in Kentucky as the property of Mr. Shelby, a kindhearted planter. George escapes from his owner, the cruel Mr. Harris, planning to buy his wife and son their freedom later. But when Eliza learns that circumstances have forced Shelby to sell Harry and Tom, she flees with her son. Haley, the slave trader who has purchased the two slaves, transports Tom down the Mississippi River. During the trip, Tom saves the life of a white six-year-old girl named Eva, whose father, Augustine St. Clare, then buys him.

The wealthy New Orleans plantation owner treats Tom well, and Tom be-

Frederick Douglass, an escaped slave, was one of America's most powerful voices for abolition. His first autobiography made a deep impression on Harriet Beecher Stowe.

friends Eva, who falls ill and eventually dies. When St. Clare dies soon afterward, his slaves are put up for auction and Tom falls into the hands of Simon Legree, an evil master originally from New England. On Legree's Louisiana plantation Tom suffers all kinds of abuses and indignities, yet he remains patient and good throughout. Meanwhile George, Eliza, and Harry reunite and cross over the Canadian border to freedom. Tom, by contrast, meets a cruel fate. Legree orders him beaten to death just before George Shelby, the son of Tom's first master, arrives to buy him back. When he learns what has happened to Tom, George renounces slavery and takes up the cause of abolition.

In constructing *Uncle Tom's Cabin* Stowe recalled thousands of details that she had, in her "extraordinary little vaguely observant, slightly wool-gathering, letting her eyes wander all over the place kind of little way," as novelist Henry James put it, carefully stored in her memory over the years. Many of the characters and incidents described in *Uncle Tom's Cabin* had their basis in actual people and events. Dozens of abolitionists, slaves, and slave owners that she had met or heard about appeared in its pages, sometimes as parts of composite characters.

Eliza, for instance, escapes by carrying her son across the Ohio River on ice floes and following the Under-

Abolitionists help slaves escape along the Underground Railroad. The secret network smuggled slaves out of the South and hid them from slave hunters.

ground Railroad to Canada. She had her model in a fugitive woman who actually fled Kentucky in the same way and settled in Toronto, Ontario. The reason for Eliza's flight—her fear of being separated from her child by his sale to a new owner—was a situation of which Stowe had read and heard often. The writer had actually witnessed a scene on the Cincinnati waterfront in which a slave family was broken up by a slave trader who sold the father to one buyer, the mother to another, and their three-year-old child to a third. Events like this convinced

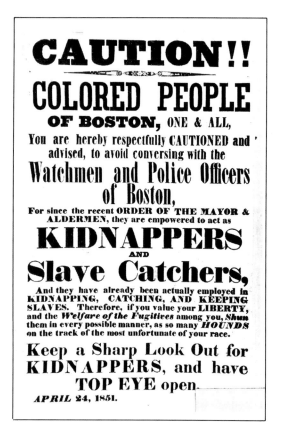

A placard posted by abolitionists warns Boston's blacks to avoid law enforcement officers, whom the Fugitive Slave Act empowered to capture runaway slaves.

Harriet Beecher Stowe created a virtuous slave as the protagonist of Uncle Tom's Cabin. *This illustration shows Tom rescuing little Eva from drowning.*

Stowe that the instability of the slave family constituted one of the great miseries of life in bondage.

While composing her story, Stowe wrote to Frederick Douglass requesting information on plantation life "from one who has been an actual laborer on one." She also scoured her memory for details observed during her 1833 Kentucky plantation visit. After *Uncle Tom's Cabin* was published,

Mary Dutton, Stowe's companion on that trip, recalled that at the time Stowe had not seemed "to notice anything in particular that happened, but sat much of the time as though abstracted in thought. When the negroes did funny things and cut up capers, she did not seem to pay the slightest attention to them." But Dutton reported that "in reading 'Uncle Tom' I recognized scene after scene of that visit portrayed with the most minute fidelity, and knew at once where the material for that portion of the story had been gathered."

When Stowe wrote of the sexual exploitation of slave women by their owners, she recorded fact. Eliza Buck, one of Stowe's housekeepers in Cincinnati, had told her about the atrocities of the slave system, describing lashings, beatings, and endless toil. The former slave shocked Stowe with the information that her children had all been fathered by her white master in Kentucky. "You know, Mrs. Stowe," she said plainly, "slave women cannot help themselves." Stowe revealed particularly strong feelings for slave women throughout *Uncle Tom's Cabin*. Indeed, her own experience of oppression as a woman—by poverty, illness, and housework—probably gave her a better understanding of slave life than that of many white male abolitionists and lent authenticity to her work.

By including some autobiographical material in *Uncle Tom's Cabin*, Stowe made the story even more believable. Less than two years after losing her own son in a cholera epidemic, she wrote of another mother coping with the death of a child. Mrs. Bird, a character who helps hide the fugitive Eliza, gives some of her dead infant's clothing to Eliza for Harry. While sorting through the items, Mrs. Bird "sat down by the drawer, and, leaning her head on her hands over it, wept till the tears

Stowe identified with slave women such as Sojourner Truth, who once asked: "I could work as much and eat as much as a man ... and bear the lash as well! And ain't I a woman?"

fell through her fingers into the drawer." In describing Mrs. Bird as one of those "blessed souls, whose sorrows all spring up into joy for others; whose earthly hopes, laid in the grave with many tears, are the seed from which spring healing flowers and balm for the desolate and the distressed," Stowe might have been speaking of herself.

The character of Eliza, who escaped Kentucky on the ice floes of the Ohio River, was based on an actual woman who had fled slavery in the same way.

Uncle Tom's Cabin derived some of its power from its portrayal of blacks as individuals with whom white readers could identify. Most of today's readers find the book racist in its patronizing attitude towards its black characters, but in 1852 *Uncle Tom's Cabin* made a radical statement concerning the dignity and courage of blacks. When slave hunters surround George and Eliza Harris, for instance, George asserts, "I am George Harris. A Mr. Harris, of Kentucky, did call me his property. But now I am a free man, standing on God's free soil." In referring to George's

"declaration of independence" as an act of heroism, Stowe made a daring pronouncement in an age when many whites believed that blacks were not human beings.

In Tom, Stowe created another kind of hero, one who followed the moral principles of loving others, "turning the other cheek," and forgiving those who did him harm. The deeply religious author believed that, by creating an impeccably virtuous slave as her book's protagonist, she could strike a mighty blow against slavery. Stowe contrasted Tom's purity with the depravity of the slave system and forced her readers to confront the injustice of holding good people in bondage.

At the end of *Uncle Tom's Cabin* Stowe offers "Concluding Remarks," a chapter in which she addresses the reader. "And now, men and women of America, is this [slavery] a thing to be trifled with, apologized for, and passed over in silence?" she asks. "Does not every American . . . owe to the African race some effort at reparation for the wrongs the American nation has brought upon them?" In her final paragraphs, Stowe tells her readers that "every nation that carries in its bosom great and unredressed injustice has in it the elements of [its] last convulsion," and warns that "injustice and cruelty shall bring on nations the wrath of Almighty God!"

The rich detail of *Uncle Tom's Cabin*, its basis in fact, and the conviction with which Stowe wrote it made the novel a compelling antislavery tract.

Tom's death at the hands of the sadistic Simon Legree both touched and enraged 19th-century readers, winning many to the cause of abolition.

Almost as soon as it appeared, *Uncle Tom's Cabin* fanned the flames of the slavery conflict and made Harriet Beecher Stowe an international celebrity.

Uncle Tom's Cabin spurred debate over slavery, made Harriet Beecher Stowe one of the most famous women of her day, and ended the Stowes' financial worries.

FIVE

"Shaking the World"

"**N**ot read Mrs. Stowe's book! But you *must*," Elizabeth Barrett Browning wrote of *Uncle Tom's Cabin*. Like millions of others—renowned literary figures, abolitionists, and ordinary people—the great English romantic poet judged *Uncle Tom's Cabin* a masterpiece. She wrote to a friend:

> Her book is quite a sign of the times, and has otherwise an intrinsically considerable power. For myself, I rejoice in the success both as a woman and a human being. Oh, and it is possible that you think a woman has no business with questions like the question of slavery. Then she had better use a pen no more. She had better subside into slavery and concubinage herself, I think . . . and take no rank among thinkers and speakers.

As 1852 wore on, sales of *Uncle Tom's Cabin* mounted into the hundreds of thousands, and Harriet Beecher Stowe heard words of extravagant praise from all over the world. "It is one of the greatest triumphs recorded in literary history, to say nothing of the higher triumph of its moral effect," wrote American poet Henry Wadsworth Longfellow. German poet Heinrich Heine called Stowe's novel the greatest book since the Bible; British historian Thomas Babington Macaulay considered it "the most valuable addition that America has made to English literature." From France, novelist George Sand wrote: "It is no longer permissible to those who can read not to have read it." Stowe, she said, "has genius . . . the genius of goodness, not that of the man of letters, but of the saint. Yes—a saint!"

Hardly anyone in the American South would have called Stowe a saint. Most white Southerners regarded

Romantic poet Elizabeth Barrett Browning considered Stowe's novel a triumph, both as an instrument of social reform and as a work of literature.

Uncle Tom's Cabin as an ignorant, malicious assault on their "peculiar institution." Its author, seethed an Alabama paper, must be "either a very bad or a very fanatical person," and Virginia school children learned to chant:

> Go, go, go
> Harriet Beecher Stowe
> We don't want you here in Virginny
> Go, go, go

One young woman, born in New Orleans the year *Uncle Tom's Cabin*

was published, remembered it as the "hideous, black, dragonlike book that hovered on the horizon of every Southern child." Some Southern authorities attempted to ban the novel, and in certain regions it was hazardous to own or display a copy. A mob ran a Mobile, Alabama, bookseller out of town for stocking it in his store, and Stowe began to leave her return address off correspondence sent to a cousin who wintered in Georgia. The cousin had asked her to do so, fearing what her neighbors might do if they found out that she was related to the infamous author.

Southern writers sprang to slavery's defense, publishing numerous articles, stories, and poems in response to *Uncle Tom's Cabin*. They gave their works titles like *Aunt Phyllis's Cabin; or Southern Life as It Is* and *Black Diamonds Gathered in the Darkey Homes of the South*. Portraying plantation life as easy and relations between slaves and their owners as friendly, Southern authors attempted to disprove Stowe's assertion that blacks suffered under slavery. In his poem *The Hireling and the Slave*, South Carolinian William J. Grayson cites the joys of slave life:

> And Christian slaves may challenge as
>   their own,
> The blessings claimed in fabled states
>   alone—
> The cabin home, not comfortless,
>   though rude,
> Light daily labor, and abundant food,

Uncle Tom's Cabin *fanned the flames of the conflict over slavery. In the tense atmosphere, abolitionist debates sometimes turned into brawls.*

The sturdy health that temperate habits
　　yield,
The cheerful song that rings in every
　　field,
The long, loud laugh that freemen sel-
　　dom share,
Heaven's boon to bosoms unapproached
　　by care.

According to proslavery writers, blacks were a happy but hopelessly inferior people who benefited from the protection of their owners and the security of the slavery system. Freed slaves, incapable of caring for themselves, lived miserable lives, claimed many of these authors. Grayson's poem mourns the fate of blacks in the North,

where, he said, " . . . in suburban dens and human sties, In foul excesses sunk, the Negro lies." In this view, blacks were better off as slaves because "a nigger can't be anything but a nigger," as a black character in Sarah Josepha Hale's *Liberia* put it.

While anti-*Uncle Tom* literature fueled the spread of abolitionist feeling in the North, the antislavery furor created by *Uncle Tom's Cabin* and its fallout fed Southern anger. Nearly every day the Stowes received obscene, anonymous hate mail with Southern postmarks. Calvin Stowe, for instance, once unwrapped a small parcel ad-

UNCLE TOM'S CABIN

TOWERING ABOVE ITS CONTEMPORARIES

NO AMERICAN PLAY HAS EVER BEEN SO ENTHUSIASTICALLY RECEIVED

A GRAND PLAY SUPERBLY PRESENTED
BY AN EXCELLENT COMPANY.

DEATH OF EVA.

A Wonderful Story by a Wonderful Woman—Harriet Beecher Stowe, whose name and fame have been handed down, and as long as her as long as children will come forward to the affairs of life, generation after generation of Beecher or Stowe is spoken to presently known to public affair or to history, as long as the colored race exists—just as long as Mrs. Stowe's work be read and endeared to the future as in the past.

UNCLE TOM'S CABIN

is not simply an amusement, it is a drama of our country, and the only one that is a part of our Nation's History.

TAKE THE CHILDREN

And give them an ideal and lasting lesson in American history.

IT IS DELIGHTFUL, WONDERFUL, INSTRUCTIVE AND MORAL.

Countless stage versions of Stowe's story were presented in the years preceding the Civil War. Most sensationalized its plot and depicted blacks as simpletons.

dressed to his wife which contained an ear severed from the head of a slave. The vehemence of Southern outrage genuinely surprised Harriet Beecher Stowe, because she had worked hard to present a balanced, credible picture of slavery. Hoping to show that the institution, and not necessarily the people involved in it, was immoral, she had portrayed both good and evil Northerners and Southerners. Stowe had expected her approach to the issue of slavery to win Southern acclaim and provoke Northern criticism.

Instead, Stowe's treatment of slavery, moderate as it was, had the opposite effect. *Uncle Tom's Cabin* made its author one of the North's—and the world's—most admired women. "How she is shaking the world with her *Uncle Tom's Cabin!*" poet Henry Wadsworth Longfellow confided to his diary. With more than a trace of envy, he wrote of her success, "At one step she has reached the top of the staircase up which the rest of us climb on our knees year after year." Stowe could not have stopped the growth of her fame if she had wanted to. British, French, German, Russian, and other foreign editions of *Uncle Tom's Cabin* sold out almost as soon as they appeared; toys and games based on the book were popular; and scores of theater production companies presented their own versions of the story.

The stage versions of *Uncle Tom's Cabin* bore little resemblance to the novel and were designed solely to make money for their producers. Stowe had no direct involvement in any of them and never received a dime

THE FAMOUS JARRETT & PALMER LONDON COMPY SLAVINS ORIGINAL AMERICAN TROUPE

CONSOLIDATED WITH

UNCLE TOM'S CABIN.

Attracted by dramatic gimmicks, such as fierce dogs, not found in the original Uncle Tom's Cabin, *millions who never read the book saw stage versions of the story.*

in royalties. The productions usually retained the most dramatic elements of the plot but softened the story's antislavery message. The familiar characters appeared, but were reduced to stereotypes, with white actors in blackface usually playing the parts of black characters.

Where Stowe had described Uncle Tom as powerful and intelligent, onstage he became a childish old man, stupid and cowardly, who compulsively danced to banjo music. To attract patrons, competing theater companies added gimmicks such as "a pack of genuine bloodhounds," "African mandolin players," "Tinker the famous trick donkey," and minstrels who sang such tunes as "Happy Are We, Darkies So Gay," and "Uncle Breve Tells About the Good Times He Had on the Old Plantation." Audiences loved the spectacles, and millions who never read *Uncle Tom's Cabin* saw some version of it on the stage.

Though distressed by the burlesques, Stowe was happy to discover that fame had its rewards. In May 1852

The Stowes moved into this stone house in Andover, Massachusetts, when Calvin Stowe accepted a teaching position at the Theological Seminary there.

she treated herself to a visit to New York and a stay with her brother Henry Ward Beecher and found herself pampered as a celebrity. When she found that tickets to a concert by Jenny Lind, the famed "Swedish Nightingale," had been sold out for months, she enjoyed a first taste of the privileges of rank. Through a wealthy, well-connected friend of her brother, she obtained two tickets for the best seats in the house.

The success of *Uncle Tom's Cabin* also ended the Stowes' perennial worries about money. In the summer of 1852 Stowe received her first royalty payment of $10,300, an enormous sum at the time. The checks would pour in for years to come, ending the days of poverty for good, but though they now lived comfortably, the pious Stowes never let wealth or fame go to their heads. "It is not fame nor praise that contents me," Stowe wrote to her husband. "I seem never to have needed love so much as now."

Calvin Stowe had met with good fortune as well. In 1852 he was appointed professor of sacred literature at the Theological Seminary in Andover, Massachusetts, with a salary double that paid him at Bowdoin. The family moved to Andover in late summer and set up housekeeping in an old stone building, formerly a coffin factory, that they had renovated. There they would live, "human and hearty and happy," according to a neighbor, for the next 12 years.

During her first winter in Andover, Stowe formulated her response to Southern charges that she knew nothing of the slave system. She worked all winter compiling the sources she had used in writing *Uncle Tom's Cabin* and other evidence that supported her depiction of life in the South. In the spring of 1853 she published *A Key to Uncle Tom's Cabin*, a defense of her novel. The book sold well—more than 100,000 copies—but was not widely read in the South, where she had hoped it would satisfy her critics.

After writing the *Key*, Stowe took her first trip to Europe, at the invitation of the Glasgow, Scotland, Anti-Slavery Society, which offered to pay all the expenses for both her and her husband. On March 30, 1853, the Stowes set sail from Boston on the steamer

The citizens of Edinburgh, Scotland, held a lavish banquet in honor of Stowe when the antislavery writer visited their city in 1853.

Niagara. An 11-day voyage brought them to Liverpool, England, where a large crowd greeted them on the pier. As they rode through the streets, clusters of people on the sidewalks waved, called out, and tipped their hats to the famous author.

The enthusiastic reception portended a sensationally triumphant tour of Great Britain. Britain had abolished slavery in 1838, but abolitionist feeling still ran high in England and Scotland, where organizations agitated for slavery's end in the United States. Wherever Stowe appeared, crowds strained to get a glimpse of her. Nearly 10,000 gathered outside the cathedral of Glasgow when she attended a service there. The acclaim nearly turned her head. During an excursion through the English countryside she was delighted to hear the cheers of "the plain common people," as she put it in *Sunny Memories of Foreign Lands*, her 1854 memoir of the trip. "The butcher came out of his stall and the baker from his shop, the miller dusty with flour, the blooming comely young mother, with that hearty, intelligent, friendly look as if they knew we should be glad to see them."

Stowe also traveled to London and

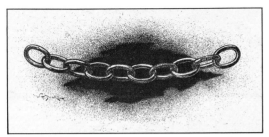

During Stowe's visit to the British Isles, the Duchess of Sutherland presented the author with a bracelet in the form of slave's manacles.

Edinburgh to speak with abolitionists, who honored the American whose novel had done so much for the anti-slavery cause. The author met with schoolchildren, working people, scholars, and nobles, including such prominent figures as the prime minister, the archbishop of Canterbury, author Charles Dickens, and political leaders William Gladstone and Lord Palmerston. She collected more than $20,000 for the American abolitionist movement, and at one of her stops, she received 26 leather-bound volumes containing "An Affectionate Christian Address from the Women of Great Britain to the Women of America." The letter, calling for the end of slavery in the United States, was signed by more than half a million women from throughout the British Empire.

At the end of May, Calvin Stowe returned home while Harriet Beecher Stowe and her brother Charles Beecher traveled on to continental Europe, where they planned to tour France, Switzerland, and Germany. Stowe was not as well known on the continent, so she enjoyed more ordinary tourist pastimes there, visiting museums, cathedrals, mountains, and lakes. The straitlaced New Englander found Paris both shocking and irresistible: At a popular night spot, for instance, she was aghast that men and women let their bodies touch when dancing, but after her initial surprise she admitted that she rather liked the carefree atmosphere. Stowe relished all her new experiences in Europe, but grew increasingly homesick. In September she and her brother sailed for America.

Upon her return from Europe, Stowe discovered that she remained a controversial figure in America. She heard more criticism of her antislavery activities, such as that leveled by a minstrel singer in blackface:

But don't come back, Aunt Harriet; in
 England make a fuss,
Go talk against your country, put your
 money in your puss;
And when us happy darkies you pity in
 your prayer,
Oh, don't forget de WHITE SLAVES dat's
 starvin' ober dar!

The reference to "white slaves" was a common line of defense for slavery's advocates. Southerners claimed that abolitionists, in their concern for blacks, ignored the plight of poor white industrial workers in the North and in England. In their opinion, slaves were

In 1856 militant abolitionist John Brown led a guerrilla band in a massacre of proslavery settlers at Pottawatomie Creek in the territory of Kansas.

Congressman Preston Brooks flogs Senator Charles Sumner on the floor of the Senate. Violence erupted everywhere as the slavery controversy intensified.

no worse off than these workers, who were paid miserable wages for long hours of backbreaking labor. Abolitionists, of course, held that the comparison was not valid.

Tension over the slavery question rose every day, and violence erupted with greater frequency than ever before. Abolitionists publicized dramatic rescues of fugitive slaves; William Lloyd

Garrison protested slavery by burning a copy of the U.S. Constitution. The Fugitive Slave Act proved unenforceable in many Northern states; the Compromise of 1850 collapsed. In Kansas, proslavery and antislavery settlers battled over the territory's future as a free or slave state. The conflict there climaxed in the May 1856 slaughter of five proslavery settlers by fanatical abolitionist John Brown. That month Preston Brooks, a congressman from South Carolina, assaulted antislavery senator Charles Sumner of Massachusetts on the floor of the United States Senate. Slavery was tearing the country apart.

In late 1862 Harriet Beecher Stowe visited President Abraham Lincoln in the White House and urged him to sign the Emancipation Proclamation.

SIX

"This Great War"

Harriet Beecher Stowe watched as the United States descended into chaos and began to lose hope that slavery could be ended through peaceful means. Yet she still believed in abolition, and in 1856 published her second antislavery novel, *Dred: A Tale of the Great Dismal Swamp*. Stowe originally intended to take the same temperate approach to her subject that she had taken in *Uncle Tom's Cabin*, and the first half of the book has a sympathetic tone, portraying an intelligent slaveholder doing his best to treat his slaves well. But after hearing of Preston Brook's attack on Senator Sumner, a personal friend of hers, Stowe turned the book into a tale of revenge. Her tone toward Southerners became sharp, as when she described a thinly disguised version of Brooks, who "proved his eligibility for Con-

gress by beating his defenseless acquaintance on the head, after the fashion of the chivalry of South Carolina."

Dred's title character, an escaped slave, lives among other blacks hiding out in the Dismal Swamp of North Carolina. A charismatic man, possibly modeled on Nat Turner, Dred encourages the fugitives to take up arms against their former masters, prophesying a war that will liberate slaves. But Dred never leads the rebellion of which he dreams, and in the end he is shot by white slave hunters and dies in the swamp. The novel suffers from a weak, tangled plot and from its depiction of unrealistic characters for whom the reader can feel little sympathy. Many literary critics of the day called *Dred* an unworthy successor to *Uncle Tom's Cabin*, but Stowe was still popular with

On her second trip to England, Harriet Beecher Stowe met Queen Victoria and Prince Albert, shown here in 1861.

purpose meeting at a railway station," Queen Victoria and her consort, Prince Albert. "The Queen seemed really delighted to see my wife, and remarkably glad to see me for her sake," wrote Calvin Stowe. When the famous author presented copies of *Uncle Tom's Cabin* and *Dred* to Her Majesty, the queen "took one volume herself and handed the other to Prince Albert, and they were soon both very busy reading," reported Calvin Stowe. "She is a real nice little body, with exceedingly pleasant manners."

After visiting England, the Stowes spent several months in France and Italy. In their absence, the turmoil over slavery in America continued. The U.S. Supreme Court ruled against a slave named Dred Scott, who had sued for his freedom. In the *Dred Scott* decision, handed down on March 6, 1857, the court ruled that a black person could not file a lawsuit because blacks were not, and could not be, citizens. The judges also ruled that Congress could not restrict the spread of slavery into new U.S. territories. Northerners were shocked, and the rift between North and South widened still further.

the public and her second book became a best seller. Stowe felt secure in her success, writing to her husband: "One hundred thousand copies ... sold in four weeks! After that who cares what critics say?"

While *Dred* made its mark in America, Stowe returned to England with her husband. She once again met with prominent social and political figures, including, at "an accidental, done on

When the Stowes returned home in June 1857, they received more bad news. Their eldest son, 19-year-old Henry, a student at Dartmouth College, had drowned in a boating accident on the Connecticut River. Both his parents were crushed, his mother writing, "It seems selfish that I should yearn to lie down by his side, but I never knew how much I loved him until now." Henry's death brought back the depression that Stowe had not suffered since her days in Cincinnati. "I dread everything I do," she wrote. Nonetheless, she threw herself into her work, this time writing about New England life.

In 1859 Stowe published her third novel, *The Minister's Wooing*, an examination of Puritanism. The book's characters, who live in Newport, Rhode Island, during the 1790s, find that they cannot live up to Puritan doctrine, which requires the impossible of them. In the story, Stowe describes the route to salvation as a ladder from which the Puritan god "knocked out every rung ... but the highest, and then, pointing to its hopeless splendor, said to the world, 'Go up thither and be saved!'" At the age of 48, Stowe could finally voice her doubts about her father's religion.

Few other Americans, however, had their minds on the Puritans in 1859. On October 16, John Brown led another antislavery raid, this one in Harpers Ferry, Virginia (now West Virginia). Along with 21 others, he occupied the federal arsenal there and took several hostages. Brown failed to incite a rebellion among the local slaves, and after a number of gunfights and deaths, Colonel Robert E. Lee captured the agitators. The Virginia court tried and executed Brown, whose "martyrdom,"

Claiming that residents of free territory could not be slaves, Dred Scott sued for his liberty. The Supreme Court ruled that blacks had no right to initiate lawsuits.

philosopher-poet Ralph Waldo Emerson believed would "make the gallows as glorious as the cross."

Stowe, increasingly disgusted with the slaveholding South and impatient with the tolerant North, considered Brown a hero "who calmly gave up his life to a noble effort for human freedom." Having come to feel that violence was an acceptable means of working to end slavery, she admired the man who had had the courage to act on his beliefs. "His death will be mightier for that cause [abolition] than

John Brown led 21 abolitionists on an 1859 raid on the federal arsenal in Harpers Ferry, Virginia. Arrested and convicted of treason, Brown was hanged.

even his success," she wrote. Stowe began to consider the likelihood of war between the North and the South and closely observed the 1860 presidential race, the outcome of which would determine the nation's future. She supported the candidacy of Abraham Lincoln, although she had some reservations about his views on abolition.

Lincoln was elected president of the United States on November 6, 1860. In protest, South Carolina seceded from the Union on December 20, and was soon followed by Alabama, Florida, Georgia, Louisiana, Mississippi, and Texas. These seven states formed the Confederate States of America and on February 18, 1861, elected Jefferson

Davis president of the new nation. When Abraham Lincoln was inaugurated on March 4, he confronted the difficult task of dealing with the hostile Confederacy.

Only a few weeks later, Confederate forces attacked Fort Sumter in Charleston, South Carolina, which was still occupied by the Union troops that had been based there before the South seceded. Two days of fighting left the rebels in control of the fort. President Lincoln called for 75,000 Union volunteers to join the fight against the Confederacy and ordered a blockade of Southern ports. Arkansas, North Carolina, Tennessee, and Virginia seceded from the Union, while West Virginia

The battle lines of the Civil War were drawn in 1861 when Jefferson Davis was sworn in as president of the Confederacy (left) two weeks before Abraham Lincoln's inauguration as chief executive of the United States (right).

declared itself separate from Virginia and allied itself with the North. The Civil War had begun.

Harriet Beecher Stowe was glad that the North had finally taken up arms against the slaveholding South. "We of the free states of the North will fight this battle through to the end . . . ," she wrote. "Every man, woman, and child of us are of one mind to give it all to this cause." Along with most other Northerners, Stowe believed at the start of the war that the Southern insurrection would be put down with a few battles. But Union forces lost some key early engagements, includ-

ing one that took place on July 21, 1861. On that day, Union forces attacked Confederate troops at Manassas, Virginia, but the Southern soldiers received surprise reinforcements and were thus able to fend off the assault. The Union lost the first important conflict of the war, known as the First Battle of Bull Run, and the Civil War was thus destined to drag on.

Stowe viewed the Civil War as the North's crusade for emancipation, but President Lincoln did not at first espouse abolition as an aim of the war. The antislavery writer criticized Lincoln for neglecting abolition, and abo-

Rebel forces bombarded Fort Sumter, the island stronghold of Union troops in Charleston Harbor, for two days in April 1861 before taking the fortress.

litionists in Great Britain refused to endorse the Union cause. Lincoln had stated:

> My paramount object in this struggle *is* to save the Union, and is *not* either to save or destroy slavery.... What I do about slavery, and the colored race, I do because I believe it helps to save the Union; and what I forbear, I forbear because I do *not* believe it would help to save the Union.

Stowe denounced Lincoln for assigning greater importance to the restoration of the Union than to the abolition of slavery. In a magazine article, she bitterly attacked the president, composing a speech that she

imagined Jesus Christ might have made in Lincoln's place:

> My paramount object is to set at liberty them that are *bruised* and *not* either to save or destroy the Union. What I do in favor of the Union, I do because it helps to free the oppressed; what I forbear, I forbear because it does not help to free the oppressed.

Although she censured Lincoln, Stowe also castigated her former English allies for deserting the Union, the very institution she believed would bring about the end of slavery in the United States. She wrote that "the cause of freedom ... found little or no

Volunteers flock to a military recruiting office in New York City. By offering generous fees for enlistment, the Union reduced its need to draft soldiers.

support from the British" and chided England for selling battleships to the Confederacy. Britain, which had declared its neutrality at the war's outset, eventually agreed to stop the sales, but Stowe remained dissatisfied with the British position. Even when English popular opinion swung back to the Northern side, the island nation declined to back the Union officially.

While the war progressed, Stowe continued to write novels, working on two simultaneously. In 1862 she published *Agnes of Sorrento*, a romance set in Italy during the Renaissance and

inspired by her 1860 trip to Italy; and *The Pearl of Orr's Island*, a tale of life on the Maine coast. Stowe much preferred the Italian story. "I have a pleasure in writing *Agnes of Sorrento* that gilds this icy weather," she said during a cold New England winter. "I write my Maine story with a shiver, and come back to this as to a flowery home where I love to rest." The public shared her enthusiasm for *Agnes*, which sold more than 400,000 copies in the United States alone. Critics, on the other hand, found it overly sentimental and generally considered *The Pearl of Orr's*

Stonewall Jackson (with plume in hat) led Confederate troops to an important early victory in the First Battle of Bull Run, also known as Manassas.

Island a better effort. Sarah Orne Jewett, a writer who greatly admired Stowe, praised the book as "clear and perfectly original and strong."

On the battlefields, meanwhile, casualties mounted. Union soldiers tried but failed to capture Richmond, Virginia, throughout the first half of 1862, while Confederate general Stonewall Jackson engaged Northern forces in the Shenandoah Valley. At the Second Battle of Bull Run in August 1862, rebel troops again crushed Union forces. On sea, the Union navy took one Confed-

erate port—Roanoke, New Orleans, Galveston, Pensacola—after another, exacting heavy losses on both sides. The bloodiest day of the war came in September, when Confederate general Robert E. Lee invaded Union territory and met resistance at Sharpsburg, Maryland. There, at Antietam Creek, more than 24,000 soldiers were killed or wounded before Lee's troops were forced to retreat.

Stowe wrote that the "inquisition for blood has been strict and awful. . . . For every stricken household of the poor

The USS Cairo *was one of the new armored ships used in the Civil War. The use of such technology made the 19th-century conflict the first modern war.*

and lowly [North] hundreds of households of the oppressor [South] have been scattered." President Lincoln, searching for a way to end the carnage and win the war, now realized that he could strengthen the Union's position by declaring abolition a prime objective. Doing so would rally foreign support for the North and, whenever rebel territory came under the control of Union forces, provide it with fresh soldiers in the form of freed slaves. Soon after the narrow victory at Antietam, Lincoln issued a preliminary procla-

mation stating that on New Year's Day of 1863 slaves in the rebel states would be freed.

In November 1862 Stowe decided to pay a visit to the president to "satisfy myself that I may refer to the Emancipation Proclamation as a reality." She told her publisher, "I mean to have a talk with 'Father Abraham' himself." Stowe's 26-year-old daughter Harriet and 12-year-old son Charles accompanied her on the trip. Stowe sat and talked with Lincoln for an hour. The author was impressed with the presi-

The battle of Antietam, "the bloodiest single day of the war," littered the Maryland countryside with bodies, moving Lincoln to declare Southern blacks free.

dent's kindness, decency, and honest intention to free the slaves, and after their conversation she never uttered another critical word of him. Stowe told her daughter that Lincoln said upon meeting her, "So this is the little lady who made this great war."

On New Year's Day, 1863, in the midst of the Civil War, Abraham Lincoln signed the Emancipation Proclamation, which stated that "all persons held as slaves within said designated states and parts of states are, and henceforward shall be, free." The edict could not be enforced in the rebel states, where the federal government had no power, but it marked a tremendous advance in the cause of American blacks.

On the day Lincoln issued the Emancipation Proclamation, a crowd filled Boston Music Hall for a New Year's Emancipation Jubilee. Harriet Beecher Stowe arrived quietly and took a modest seat far up in the balcony to watch the proceedings. An orchestra played selections by Beethoven and Mendelssohn while the audience celebrated the end of slavery. At four o'clock in the afternoon came the announcement that the president had just signed the proclamation. The hall

Lincoln reads the Emancipation Proclamation to his cabinet. Stowe's admirers credited Uncle Tom's Cabin *with hastening the end of slavery.*

rocked with cheers. Suddenly a chant rose out of the tumult. "Mrs. Stowe! Mrs. Stowe! Mrs. Stowe!" The crowd had recognized the author and now pressed in around her. Someone led Stowe to the balcony rail. When the entire audience could see her, the chanting stopped and waves of applause thundered through the house.

Harriet Beecher Stowe could only bow and wipe away her tears.

The acclaim would ring forever in Stowe's ears, and New Year's Day, 1863, would live forever in America's memory. But the divided nation was still at war, and in the rebel states, blacks still lived in bondage. Stowe would not be satisfied until every slave was free.

Fred Stowe, injured while fighting in the Union army, became an alcoholic. For eight years his mother tried to find a cure, but Fred vanished in 1871.

SEVEN

Peace and Controversy

Change was coming rapidly not only to the nation but also to Harriet Beecher Stowe's family. Eighty-seven-year-old Lyman Beecher died in early 1863. "The old oak finally fell," Henry Ward Beecher wired his sister. Stowe mourned the passing of the man who had had such a profound influence on her life, but she had long since rejected her father's harsh, fire-and-brimstone brand of religion. In a few years she would formalize the break with her father's faith and begin worshipping in the Episcopal church.

Only a few months after Lyman Beecher's death, Stowe nearly lost her 21-year-old son Frederick. Fred Stowe had been one of the first young men to enlist in the Union army's infantry. As an abolitionist, Stowe took considerable pride in his dedication to the Union cause; as a mother, however,

she feared for his safety. Her apprehensions proved well-founded in July 1863, two years after his enlistment, when he was seriously wounded during the Battle of Gettysburg.

This Pennsylvania contest represented a turning point in the Civil War. After three days of bloody fighting, victorious Union troops managed to halt a Confederate advance into the North. Seven thousand men died during the battle, and Fred Stowe nearly became one of them when he was struck in the head by a shell fragment. The wound was painfully slow in healing, and his worried mother finally pulled some strings in the War Department in order to have him medically discharged.

In November 1863 Fred Stowe rejoined his family in Andover, Massachusetts, but the homecoming proved

an unhappy one. The young man had been a heavy drinker before the war, and the situation only worsened when he returned from battle. Although disappointed in her son, Stowe never gave up hope that he would someday stop his self-destructive behavior. Over the years she encouraged him to try every possible cure for alcoholism.

Stowe's love for her husband, who retired from Andover Seminary in 1863, was a consolation during this trying period. Ever since *Uncle Tom's Cabin* had become a best-seller, the writer had been the family's principal breadwinner, but Calvin Stowe never seemed to resent being known as "Mr. Harriet Beecher Stowe." He sometimes lapsed into childishness, and even in middle age he remained emotional and impetuous. Now, as he worked fitfully on a history of the Bible, he procrastinated so often that Harriet Beecher Stowe teased him for committing "the original sin of laziness." But Calvin Stowe possessed a gentle, thoughtful nature, and when he put on a good deal of weight, let his white beard grow long, and started wearing a black skullcap, his wife fondly began calling him "my Rabbi."

With Calvin Stowe retired there was little to hold the couple in Andover.

Union forces face Confederate troops at Gettysburg. The Northern victory there marked the end of the Southern advance and presaged the war's outcome.

Stowe called her bald, bearded, and portly husband "my rabbi." The biblical scholar was pleased with the appellation.

Harriet Beecher Stowe decided they should move to Hartford, Connecticut, the scene of her happy friendships with Georgiana May and Mary Dutton. There Stowe planned to build the house of her dreams. "Four acres and a half of lovely woodland," was how she described the site, which ran along the Park River precisely where she and Georgiana May had walked and laughed so many years before. In no time gardeners and contractors had invaded the riverside, and a towering mansion started its uncertain rise. Stowe was enthusiastically involved in every stage of the project. "My house

with *eight* gables is growing wonderfully. I go over every day to see it. I am busy with drains, sewers, sinks, digging, trenching. . . ."

When it was finished, the Stowes named their new dwelling "Oakholm," although it might have been more appropriately dubbed "Stowe's Folly." The house was eccentrically designed, poorly built, expensive to maintain, and almost unlivable. The plumbing, for instance, seldom worked. One night the pipes above Calvin Stowe's bed exploded. Drenched to the skin, he reportedly fell into the hallway and sputtered, "Oh yes, all the modern conveniences! Shower baths while you sleep!" Furthermore, Harriet Beecher Stowe had been so determined to build exactly where she and her friends had walked that she was blind to the drawbacks of the location. The neighborhood was becoming an industrial slum, the Park River a sewer.

The Oakholm disaster forced Stowe to step up her already impressive literary output. She needed money to pay the mountain of bills from builders, plumbers, and landscapers. Fortunately, her articles always got top dollar from the magazines of the day. She wrote everything from biographical pieces to short stories to travelogues. Her topics covered a wide spectrum: gardening, religion, child care, financial management, decorating, even raising pets.

Stowe was saddened that one of

Oakholm, Stowe's "house with eight gables," proved an expensive mistake. The Stowes lived in the impractical house only briefly.

these pieces was an obituary. President Abraham Lincoln was shot by John Wilkes Booth on Good Friday, April 14, 1865, and died the following morning. Stowe wrote: "His were the cares, the watching, the toils, the agonies, of a nation in mortal struggle; and God, looking down, was so well pleased with his humble faithfulness ... that earthly rewards and honors seemed all too poor for him, so He reached down and took him to immortal glories."

Lincoln's assassination coincided with the final days of the Civil War. Confederate general Robert E. Lee, worn down by a devastating offensive led by Union general Ulysses S. Grant, surrendered on April 9; rebel troops under General Joseph E. Johnston surrendered to Union general William T. Sherman five days later. Stowe was saddened by the enormous cost of the war—an estimated 620,000 had died on both sides—yet she was thrilled by the Union victory. The Southern rebellion crushed, Congress enacted the Thirteenth Amendment to the Constitution, outlawing slavery for good, that December.

Stowe eulogized Lincoln after his assassination, writing, "his were the cares, the watching, the toils, the agonies, of a nation in mortal struggle."

Harriet Beecher Stowe was 54 years old when the reunited American republic finally freed the women, men, and children who had served as its slaves. She had looked forward to this momentous event for decades, but concern for her son clouded her joy over its arrival. Frederick Stowe was still drinking to excess, and his mother had become desperate to help him overcome his alcoholism.

One day Fred came home filled with enthusiasm for Florida. Some of his barroom friends had been telling him of the cheap land, inexpensive labor, and endless opportunity there. Reasoning that hard work and fresh air might help him overcome his drinking problem, Stowe decided to help him begin a new life in the South. She rented Laurel Grove, a 1,000-acre cotton plantation on the Saint John's River, and installed Fred as its manager. In the early spring of 1867 she visited him there for the first time and was pleased with what she saw. There was still a great deal of work to be done on the plantation, but Fred Stowe was tanned, happy, and best of all, sober.

A year later Stowe returned to Florida, but this sojourn was not as pleasant as her first. Traveling through Virginia and the Carolinas, Stowe witnessed firsthand the devastation that the Civil War had brought the South. Flourishing cities had been destroyed, rich farmlands had been laid waste, and families had been torn apart by the deaths of sons and fathers. Local residents courteously, if a bit uncomfortably, greeted the abolitionist author of *Uncle Tom's Cabin*. Stowe was shaken by her journey, and things only grew worse when she arrived in Florida. The plantation had failed, and Fred Stowe was in a drunken stupor. The unsuccessful Laurel Grove venture cost the Stowes $10,000.

Financial necessity drove Harriet Beecher Stowe to write, in addition to countless magazine articles, 10 books between 1863 and 1870. Her published work ranged from children's stories to

The brilliant, aggressive campaigns of Union general Ulysses S. Grant helped bring the North to victory. The military hero became America's 18th president.

Lee surrenders to Grant at Appomattox, Virginia. The Union victory ensured passage of the Thirteenth Amendment, which guaranteed liberty for American blacks.

volumes of religious poetry, and most of these efforts have been dismissed by critics as hackwork. Some of the books she produced during this period began as series of magazine pieces. *Men of Our Times*, published in 1868, consists of 18 sketches of "leading patriots of the day." These included President Lincoln, escaped slave and abolitionist speaker Frederick Douglass, and Union general Ulysses S. Grant, who was elected president in 1868. Stowe's brother Henry Ward Beecher was another one of the men profiled in the work, and she presented a sympa-

thetic, personal portrait of the well-known clergyman and reformer.

The following year Stowe published one of her most highly regarded novels, *Oldtown Folks*. A masterful, amusing portrait of New England life in bygone days, the book was based on her husband's vivid stories about his hometown of Natick, Massachusetts. "I would endeavor to show you," Stowe wrote in the book's preface, "New England in its *seed-bed*, before the hot suns of modern progress had developed its sprouting germs into the great trees of to-day." The novel's narrator had all of Calvin Stowe's traits, and Parson Avery, "a cheerful, busy manly man," seems to be based on her father. Harriet Beecher Stowe's descriptive powers were at their peak in *Oldtown Folks*. The town know-it-all is characterized as "a gnarly, compact, efficient little pepperbox of a woman, with a mouth always at half-cock ready to go off with some crack."

Unwilling to abandon her hopes for the recovery of her son—and of the South—Stowe bought a 200-acre orange grove in Mandarin, Florida, a year after the Laurel Grove disaster. The land bordered the Saint John's, which she called "the most magnificent river in America." There Fred Stowe had another chance to redeem himself through work, and his parents spent their winters with him, enjoying the subtropical climate and working to improve the lot of the area's recently liberated blacks. Harriet Beecher Stowe spent her time sailing, picnicking, and raising money for a variety of causes, particularly the local church and school. Her husband spent most of the day in his porch rocking chair, and on Sundays he held services for both black and white worshipers.

The couple soon felt at home in Mandarin, often spending as much as six months a year there. As she enjoyed the soothing effect of Florida's mild weather, Stowe began to wonder what impact the balmy climate might have had on the stern, unyielding religion of her forebears. "How do you think New

Mourning women contemplate the ruins of Richmond, Virginia. On a trip through the South, Stowe was shocked to witness the devastation the war had wrought.

England theology would have fared," she mused, "if our fathers had landed here instead of Plymouth Rock?" Drawing on her experiences and observations in Florida, Stowe wrote a series of sketches for a newspaper called the *Christian Union*. The series appeared in 1873 as a book with the title *Palmetto-Leaves*.

Harriet Beecher Stowe, the famous Northern abolitionist, had embraced life in the South—and the South returned her affections. Northerners, drawn by her vivid, glowing reports of Florida's delightful climate and good-natured population, visited the state in droves, and the Stowes themselves became a tourist attraction. Postcards depicting them at their winter home were sold across the country. A local company promoted tours that featured a view of the Stowe orange groves and offered patrons the opportunity to catch a glimpse of the nation's most famous author. What these eager visitors usually saw, however, was Calvin Stowe angrily waving his cane at them from the front porch. But although they often found themselves beleaguered by curious visitors, the Stowes were pleased that the tourism they generated helped the local economy.

Stowe had generally stayed away from controversy since the Civil War, but in 1869 and 1870 she once again risked her reputation to stand up for her beliefs. But whereas *Uncle Tom's Cabin* had lifted her to the loftiest heights a writer can reach, her exposé of her childhood idol, acclaimed British Romantic poet Lord Byron, nearly ruined her public image.

During her 1856 visit to England, Stowe had become a close friend of mathematician Anne Isabella Milbanke Byron, the widow of Lord Byron. Lady and Lord Byron had been married only a year before she left him, returning to her parents' house with their infant daughter. It was commonly believed that Lady Byron had made the poet's life miserable when they lived together and had wronged him greatly by leaving him and taking away his child. After their separation, Lord Byron had left for the European continent, where he gambled, pursued a string of lovers, and drank heavily. Many people blamed his descent into a dissolute life on the wounds inflicted by Lady Byron.

When Stowe first met Lady Byron, the poet had been dead for more than 30 years. A spark of intimate friendship was struck between the two women, and Lady Byron decided to confide in her American friend. She confirmed some rumors, which Stowe had already heard, that it was actually Lord Byron who had ruined their marriage. The image of the great, noble Lord Byron was a sham, his widow maintained. In actuality he had been a philandering drunkard long before they had met, a depraved man who had even had an incestuous relationship with his half sister.

Lady Byron died a few years after Stowe returned to the United States. In 1868 Byron's last mistress, Countess Teresa Guiccioli, published a memoir that blamed Lady Byron for the poet's exile from Great Britain, his unhappiness, even his death. Stowe found these charges especially infuriating because Anne Byron was no longer able to defend her honor. To reclaim her friend's good name, she decided to write and publish Anne Byron's story of Lord Byron's conduct, including his shocking relationship with his half sister. Calvin Stowe begged her to reconsider, warning her that the article would stir up a hornet's nest of criti-

Two visitors flank the Stowes in the front yard of their Florida home. The aging couple enjoyed wintering in the mild Southern climate.

In this cartoon attacking Stowe for defaming Lord Byron, Uncle Tom asks, "After painting a nigger like me so white, how could she paint one of her own brethren so black?"

cism. But Harriet Beecher Stowe remained fiercely determined that Lady Byron's account should come out. In the fall of 1869 the *Atlantic Monthly* carried her article, "The True Story of Lady Byron's Life."

Perhaps Stowe should have heeded her husband's warnings. Most 19th-century Americans were prudish about sex, and they reacted as if she had written a piece of pornography. The *Atlantic* promptly lost 15,000 subscribers just for printing the piece, but its author drew the brunt of the criti-

cism. Newspapers accused her of being a vulgar, scandal-mongering gossip. *Gentlemen's Magazine* published a parody of her article entitled "Mrs. Shakespeare's Life," supposedly written by "a descendant of Harriet B. Cherstow." An indignant U.S. congressman proclaimed that "nothing from her pen is considered reliable by the American public." And across the Atlantic Ocean, England's House of Commons debated barring Stowe from the British Isles for defaming one of their national heroes.

Although most of the criticism attacked Stowe personally, some of it questioned her version of the facts. One London newspaper asserted that she had made her charges "without authority, and without confirmatory proof." Stowe felt that she had all the proof she needed—Lady Byron's word. Instead of being cowed by her critics, she resolved to fight back.

In 1870 Stowe expanded her article into a book entitled *Lady Byron Vindicated*. This volume further developed her portrait of Lord Byron as an abusive, mentally unsound husband. Some readers and critics supported her conclusions, but as with the article, the response was overwhelmingly unfavorable. One British academic even branded her work "an odious narrative, serving the cause of neither literature nor morality." American poet Edmund Clarence Stedman called Lady Byron "a jealous virtuous prude" and Stowe "a gossiping green old granny."

But Stowe was sure of the fairness of her account of Lord Byron's life, a confidence that has been borne out by modern historians, who generally agree that Lady Byron's charges were just. Even when the criticism was at its height, Stowe never regretted writing either the article or the book on the Byrons. As she told Horace Greeley, editor of the New York *Tribune*, "I

Despite criticism leveled against her, Stowe (pictured) stood by her defense of Lady Byron, whom she believed was unjustly blamed for Lord Byron's failings.

consider Lady Byron's story as a type of the old idea of woman: that is, a creature to be crushed and trodden under foot whenever her fate and that of a man come in conflict." Just as she had been moved to action by injustices committed against blacks, she knew she could not stand by when they were perpetrated against women.

In her final years, Harriet Beecher Stowe enjoyed the company of her children and grandchildren and the admiration of her colleagues.

EIGHT

"Favored Among Women"

In 1871, as the storm over *Lady Byron Vindicated* gradually died down, Harriet Beecher Stowe turned 60. She and her husband continued to enjoy their winters in Mandarin, and during the summer and fall Hartford was home. After the Oakholm disaster, the Stowes had moved into a modest house with bay windows, walnut woodwork, and room to play croquet in the backyard. The city of Hartford was a literary center at the time, and the Stowes' next-door neighbor was the up-and-coming writer Samuel Langhorne Clemens, better known as Mark Twain.

Harriet Beecher Stowe's life revolved around her family during these years. Her eldest children, the twins Eliza and Harriet, still lived at home. Neither had married and both devoted themselves to looking after their parents. The Stowes' youngest daughter, Georg-

iana, had married an Episcopal minister and in 1870 gave birth to Calvin and Harriet's first grandchild, a little boy named Freeman. The youngest Stowe, Charles, followed a career path similar to his forebears. He had gone to Harvard University, entered the clergy, and now preached at a church in Hartford.

But Fred Stowe's life was careening toward disaster. Unable to control his drinking, he gave into despair. "I would kill myself and end it all," he told his mother one day, "but I know that you and all the family would feel the disgrace that such an end would bring upon you." In 1871 Fred Stowe sailed around South America's Cape Horn to Chile and, finally, to California. He disembarked in San Francisco and was never heard from again. The police never found any trace of him, but his

97

The Stowes settled into this modest Hartford, Connecticut, house following the Oakholm fiasco. There, their two unmarried daughters cared for them.

mother never gave up hope that he would return.

The following year Harriet Beecher Stowe faced yet another family crisis, one that centered around her brother, Henry Ward Beecher. By the early 1870s he was a public institution, the most popular and influential clergyman and reformer in the country. A mesmerizing orator, he enthralled a generation of audiences. One of the thousands of listeners he impressed was Mark Twain, who reported that Beecher "went marching up and down the stage waving his arms in the air, hurling sarcasms this way and that, discharging rockets of poetry, and exploding mines of eloquence, halting now and then to stamp his foot three times in succession to emphasize a point." There was never an empty pew at the Plymouth Church in Brooklyn, New York, when Beecher gave his sermons. During his lecture tours of the United States and Great Britain he commanded the highest fees. He was

Mark Twain, Stowe's Hartford neighbor, called Uncle Tom's Cabin *"a drama which will live as long as the English tongue shall live."*

known as a champion of a variety of causes, from the antislavery movement to the battle for woman suffrage. At his stylish estate in the suburbs of New York he and his wife entertained some of the best-known public figures of the day and raised 10 children. Henry Ward Beecher seemed, in short, about the least likely person to stand trial for adultery.

Beecher's fortunes began to turn when he publicly insulted Victoria Woodhull, an advocate of women's rights and "free love," the idea that sexual relations outside of marriage were morally acceptable. Beecher called Woodhull a prostitute, and she retaliated on November 2, 1872, with a special issue of her newspaper, the *Weekly*. The publication accused Beecher of carrying on a long-term love affair with Elizabeth Tilton, the wife of Beecher's friend and close ally in the social reform movement, Theodore Tilton. Initially shocked, Reverend Tilton finally sued Beecher for adultery in 1874. Woodhull's article and Tilton's lawsuit caused a sensational scandal that was splashed across the front pages of newspapers around the country.

Harriet Beecher Stowe did not believe a word of the charges against her brother and refused to listen to any of the evidence. In her eyes, Beecher was nearly perfect, and the assault on him wounded her deeply. "This has drawn on my life, my heart's blood," she wrote as his trial dragged on. "He is myself."

Beecher was acquitted when the jury was unable to agree on a verdict in his case, but at least one member of his family was convinced of his guilt. Isabella Beecher Hooker, Harriet Beecher Stowe's half sister and a prominent champion of women's rights, was determined to denounce Beecher from the pulpit of the Plymouth Church, his

Stowe's younger brother, Henry Ward Beecher, one of the 19th century's most famous clergymen, wielded tremendous social and political influence.

Although Stowe and Hooker differed in their assessment of Henry Ward Beecher, they were in general agreement about another subject—women's rights. In 1871 a series of Stowe's magazine pieces was published in the form of a novel entitled *My Wife and I.* Stowe's distrust of activists she considered too radical—notably Victoria Woodhull—surfaced in characters such as Audacia Dangereyes, a woman of outspoken ideas and questionable morals. But Stowe's quiet feminism is evident in her flattering portraits of many of the other strong-willed, ambitious young women in the novel.

While she continued to author numerous books and articles, Stowe also launched a new career during this period. Although she had never made a speech before in her life, at the age of 61 she went on the road to give lectures. A leading booking agency had asked her to give public readings and Stowe agreed, thinking she could earn some easy money. As the time for her debut approached, however, she became increasingly nervous. Her first speaking appearance, on Friday the 13th, September 1872, was a flop. Her stage fright was apparent to all as her voice wavered and cracked. Some members of the audience walked out before she finished.

own house of worship. The family tried to talk her out of it, but she would not be deterred. Knowing that Hooker feared and idolized her, Harriet Beecher Stowe realized she might be the only one who could stop her from carrying out her threat. Stowe decided to visit Brooklyn, where she set about attending nearly every morning and evening service at Henry Ward Beecher's church. She observed her vigil from the very first pew, where she hoped to stare her brother's accuser into silence should she dare come forward. Intimidated by her formidable half sister, Isabella Beecher Hooker backed down, but Stowe never spoke to her again.

But Stowe came from a family of orators, and she refused to give up until she had improved her speaking style. The inspiration for her new, commanding approach became evident as she prepared for an important reading in Boston. Stowe playfully brushed her white hair straight up to the top of her head and called a friend to come see. "Now, my dear, gaze upon me," she said. "I am exactly like my father, when he was going to preach." According to the same friend, as Stowe read from *Uncle Tom's Cabin* later that night, the assembled crowd "could not fail to understand what her words had signified to the generation that had passed through the struggle of our war."

The next year Stowe made another tour, going as far west as Illinois. Jostling from town to town did not seem to bother her. "I never sleep better than after a long day's ride," she reported. The packed houses and roaring applause fueled her enthusiasm and enhanced her performances. "Her voice is low, just tinged with huskiness, but is quite musical," a Pittsburgh critic said of Stowe's readings. "In manner she was vivacious and gave life to many of the pages, more by suggestive action than by utterances."

Calvin Stowe missed his wife while she was off touring the country. Now in his early 70s, he was certain the end was near. Used to his hypochondria by now, in one of her letters home his wife teasingly asked that he "try to remain with us a little longer." Then, in all seriousness, she confessed, "My heart cries out for a home with you— our home together in Florida. Oh, may

Feminist publisher Victoria Woodhull fearlessly exposed Henry Ward Beecher as an adulterer. He was cleared, but present-day scholars confirm her charges.

we see it again." Motivated by her love of her husband and a desire for a much needed rest, she decided not to tour the lecture circuit for a third season, and she and her husband were reunited in Mandarin.

Although Stowe reported spending quiet days basking in the Florida sun "like a lizard," she was still not quite ready to give up writing. In 1878 she published *Poganuc People*, a warm-hearted novel based on her recollec-

Oliver Wendell Holmes wrote to Stowe, "Favored among women you are to be chosen by both sexes to hold their hearts in your hand and turn them inside out!"

tions of childhood. The author's mixed feelings about her father, Lyman Beecher, assert themselves in her descriptions of a minister character in the book, a just but hard man who is too involved in his religious musings to pay much attention to his young daughter.

Poganuc People was Harriet Beecher Stowe's last book. Although the 67-year-old novelist decided to put down her pen, her reading public was reluctant to accept her decision. Rumors circulated that the beloved author was working on yet another volume, but time proved these false. After a lifetime of writing both to support her family and to fight injustice, Stowe was ready to retire from the fray.

When Stowe turned 70 the *Atlantic Monthly*, which had published many of her stories over the years, honored her with a grand birthday party held on the broad lawns of a Massachusetts estate. Some of New England's most prominent residents attended. Author Oliver Wendell Holmes and poet John Greenleaf Whittier composed birthday tributes, and Henry Ward Beecher gave a short, emotional speech. Elizabeth Stuart Ward, another well-known writer, later remarked of the guest of honor, "Her dignity, her repose, a certain dreaminess ... characteristic of her, blended gently with a look of peace and unmistakable happiness."

Although she delighted in the admiration of her friends and colleagues, Stowe did not forget her original idealism. Solemnly addressing the assembled guests, she spoke of the progress Southern blacks had made since the end of slavery, and of the work that still had to be done to rectify past injustices. An optimist to the end, she advised, "Let us never doubt. Everything then thought to happen is going to happen."

Because Calvin and Harriet Beecher Stowe were both in deteriorating health by now, travel became increasingly difficult and they gave up their Florida winters in 1884. Calvin Stowe was the first to fail. "He requires personal attentions that only a wife ought to render," Stowe told a friend. But despite his illness, his mind stayed clear, and his wife welcomed their hours together. "I think," she said in 1884, "we have never enjoyed each other's society more than this winter." But despite all her efforts to nurse him back to health, Calvin Stowe died on August 6, 1886, with his wife at his bedside.

Stowe was devastated by the loss of her husband, but she continued to pursue life with all her energy. Scottish evangelist Henry Drummond was quite taken with her when he met her in 1886, describing her as "a wonderfully agile old lady, as fresh as a squirrel still, but with the face and air of a lion. I have not been so taken with any one on this side of the Atlantic." But time eventually took its toll, and Stowe suffered a mild stroke from which she never completely recovered. When she was 82 she wrote to Oliver Wendell Holmes: "I make no mental effort of any sort; my brain is tired out. . . . And now I rest me, like a moored boat, rising and falling on the water, with loosened cordage and flapping sail."

In her last years Stowe became in-

Writer James Baldwin dismissed Uncle Tom's Cabin *as racist. No one, however, can deny the book's role in freeing black Americans from slavery.*

creasingly eccentric, alternately amusing and dismaying her neighbors. She grew confused and at times childish. Mark Twain, still her neighbor in Hartford, reported how she liked to "come up behind a person who was deep in dreams and musings and fetch a war whoop that would jump that person out of his clothes." Even in her last years, she never gave up hope that her son Fred would return to her. She sometimes spent hours outside, picking flowers for his imagined homecoming. After years of failing health, Harriet Beecher Stowe finally succumbed to old age on July 1, 1896.

When Stowe was buried in the family plot in Andover, Massachusetts, her friends and relatives gathered by her

Novelist Henry James attributed to Harriet Beecher Stowe a unique power to move readers, not by literary technique but by the force of her convictions.

grave side and sang a hymn that Stowe herself had composed, one that reflected both her faith in God and her acceptance of death:

> It lies around us like a cloud,
> A world we do not see
> Yet the sweet closing of an eye
> May bring us there to be.

After Stowe's death, millions around the world mourned the passing of a woman whose faith, integrity, and idealism had made her one of the most celebrated humanitarians and writers of the 19th century. As poet Elizabeth Barrett Browning remarked of Stowe, "She above all women (yes, and men of the age) has moved the world—and *for good.*" In a writing career that comprised 33 books and countless articles, Stowe promoted simple virtues, celebrated the worth of all people—black and white, male and female—and above all, attacked racial injustice.

Certainly Stowe is best remembered today for *Uncle Tom's Cabin.* Her masterpiece has its detractors, and in many respects the years have been unkind to *Uncle Tom's Cabin.* Modern critics have found her plot farfetched, her characters unbelievable, and her style crudely sentimental. The character of Uncle Tom has become a sad symbol of servility: Today *Webster's Ninth New Collegiate Dictionary* defines an "Uncle Tom" as "a black who is overeager to win the approval of whites." What Stowe thought were Tom's laudable values of forgiveness and loyalty have, in some eyes, made him seem like a doormat for white feet. Novelist James Baldwin wrote in 1949 that the novel's call for reform in the South "becomes something very closely resembling the zeal of those alabaster missionaries to Africa to cover the nakedness of the natives, to hurry them into the pallid arms of Jesus and thence into slavery."

But many of the faults of *Uncle*

Tom's Cabin lie not with Stowe herself but with the impact that the mores of her time had on her thinking. When 19th-century racial stereotypes are filtered out, *Uncle Tom's Cabin* remains a book that Henry James said possessed "the large felicity of gathering in alike the small and the simple and the big and the wise, and had above all the extraordinary fortune of finding itself, for an immense number of people, much less a book than a state of vision."

That vision lives on today.

FURTHER READING

Adams, John R. *Harriet Beecher Stowe*. New York: Twayne, 1963.

Ammons, Elizabeth, ed. *Critical Essays on Harriet Beecher Stowe*. Boston: G. K. Hall, 1980.

Birdoff, Harry. *The World's Greatest Hit: Uncle Tom's Cabin*. New York: S. F. Vanni, 1947.

Crozier, Alice C. *The Novels of Harriet Beecher Stowe*. New York: Oxford University Press, 1969.

Foster, Charles H. *The Rungless Ladder: Harriet Beecher Stowe and New England Puritanism*. Durham, NC: Duke University Press, 1970.

Gerson, Noel. *Harriet Beecher Stowe*. New York: Praeger, 1976.

Johnston, Johanna. *Harriet and the Runaway Book*. New York: Harper & Row, 1977.

Kirkham, E. Bruce. *The Building of Uncle Tom's Cabin*. Knoxville: University of Tennessee Press, 1977.

McCullough, David. "The Unexpected Mrs. Stowe." In *A Sense of History: The Best Writing from the Pages of American Heritage*, edited by Byron Dobell. Boston: Houghton Mifflin, 1985.

Rourke, Constance Mayfield. *Trumpets of Jubilee: Henry Ward Beecher, Harriet Beecher Stowe, Lyman Beecher, Horace Greeley, P. T. Barnum*. New York: Harcourt, Brace, 1963.

Rouverol, Jean. *Harriet Beecher Stowe: Woman Crusader*. New York: Putnam, 1968.

Rugoff, Milton. *The Beechers: An American Family in the Nineteenth Century*. New York: Harper & Row, 1981.

Stowe, Charles Edward, ed. *The Life of Harriet Beecher Stowe Compiled from Her Letters and Journals*. Boston: Houghton Mifflin, 1889.

Stowe, Harriet Beecher. *Oldtown Folks*. New York: A.M.S. Press, 1971.

———. *Uncle Tom's Cabin*. New York: Bantam, 1981.

CHRONOLOGY

June 14, 1811	Harriet Elizabeth Beecher born in Litchfield, Connecticut
1816	Roxana Foote Beecher, mother, dies of tuberculosis
1817	Lyman Beecher, father, marries Harriet Porter
1832	Beecher family moves to Cincinnati, Ohio
1833	Beecher publishes first newspaper article; meets Calvin and Eliza Stowe
1834	Eliza Stowe dies
1836	Beecher marries Calvin Stowe
1850	Calvin and Harriet Beecher Stowe move to Brunswick, Maine
1852	Stowe publishes *Uncle Tom's Cabin*
1853	Publishes *A Key to Uncle Tom's Cabin;* travels to Europe at the invitation of the Glasgow, Scotland, Antislavery Society
1856	Publishes *Dred: A Tale of the Great Dismal Swamp*
1859	Publishes *The Minister's Wooing*
1860	Abraham Lincoln is elected president; seven Southern states secede from the Union and form the Confederate States of America
1861	Confederate forces attack Fort Sumter, marking the start of the Civil War
1862	Stowe meets with President Lincoln; publishes *Agnes of Sorrento* and *The Pearl of Orr's Island*
1863	President Lincoln signs the Emancipation Proclamation; the Stowes move to Hartford, Connecticut
1865	John Wilkes Booth assassinates Lincoln; the Civil War ends; Congress enacts the Thirteenth Amendment to the Constitution, outlawing slavery
1869	Stowe publishes *Oldtown Folks;* buys Mandarin, Florida, estate
1870	Publishes *Lady Byron Vindicated*
1872	Victoria Woodhull accuses Henry Ward Beecher, Stowe's brother, of adultery
1878	Stowe publishes *Poganuc People,* her last novel
1886	Calvin Stowe dies in Hartford
July 1, 1896	Harriet Beecher Stowe dies of old age

INDEX

INDEX

Robert E. Jakoubek is coauthor of *These United States,* an American history textbook published by Houghton Mifflin. He attended Indiana University before doing graduate research in history at Columbia University. A native of Iowa, he now lives in New York City.

Matina S. Horner is president of Radcliffe College and associate professor of psychology and social relations at Harvard University. She is best known for her studies of women's motivation, achievement, and personality development. Dr. Horner serves on several national boards and advisory councils, including those of the National Science Foundation, Time Inc., and the Women's Research and Education Institute. She earned her B. A. from Bryn Mawr College and Ph.D. from the University of Michigan, and holds honorary degrees from many colleges and universities, including Mount Holyoke, Smith, Tufts, and the University of Pennsylvania.